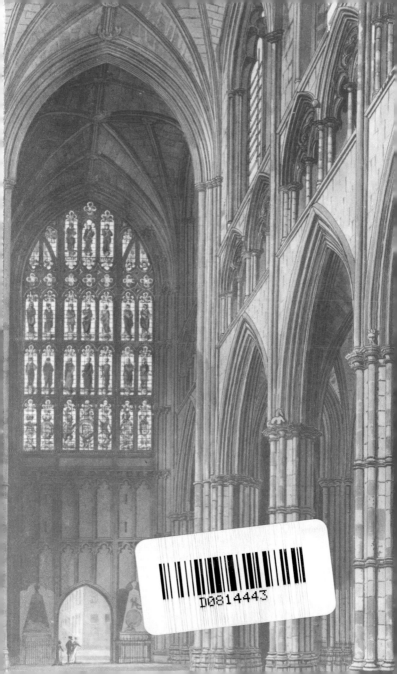

D0814443

WONDERS OF THE WORLD

WESTMINSTER ABBEY

WESTMINSTER ABBEY

RICHARD JENKYNS

HARVARD UNIVERSITY PRESS

Cambridge, Massachusetts

2005

Copyright © 2004 by Richard Jenkyns

First published in the United Kingdom in 2004 by
Profile Books Ltd
58A Hatton Garden
London ECIN 8LX

Library of Congress Cataloging-in-Publication Data

Jenkyns, Richard
Westminster Abbey / Richard Jenkyns.
p. cm.
Includes bibliographical references and index.
ISBN 0-674-01716-1 (alk. paper)
1. Westminster Abbey—History. I. Title.
DA687.W5J34 2005 283'.42132—dc22 2004054312

Printed in the United Kingdom by Butler and Tanner

CONTENTS

INTRODUCTION

Westminster Abbey is the most complex church in the world in terms of its history, functions and memories – perhaps the most complex building of any kind. It has been an abbey and a cathedral and is now a collegiate church and a royal peculiar. It is the coronation church, a royal mausoleum, a Valhalla for the tombs of the great, a 'national cathedral' and the site of the Tomb of the Unknown Warrior; in France, by contrast, these functions are divided among five separate monuments. Westminster Abbey is one of the high places of Anglicanism, but it houses the shrine of a saint of the Roman calendar, and the principles of Presbyterianism were hammered out within its walls. Its chapter house was where the Commons met in the fourteenth century, moving later to the refectory, and the treasury was in the chapter house's crypt, so that the building was Capitol and Fort Knox rolled into one. The Abbey has witnessed many strange sights: Blake saw a vision of angels in it, and Pepys used it as a place to pick up women. It is the first cemetery of the world: more of the great – whether measured by rank, office or genius – have been buried here, across a longer period, than anywhere else. It has been called the finest sculpture gallery in Britain – or even in Europe. Certainly, it contains statuary from eight centuries, and in at

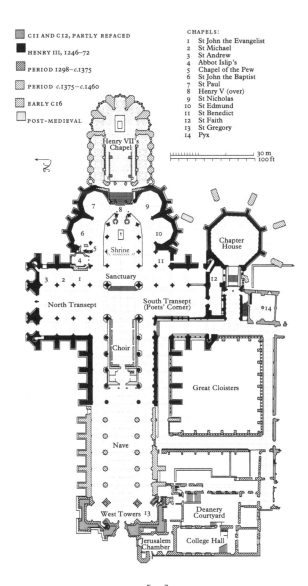

CII AND C12, PARTLY REFACED

HENRY III, 1246–72

PERIOD 1298–c.1375

PERIOD c.1375–c.1460

EARLY C16

POST-MEDIEVAL

CHAPELS:
1   St John the Evangelist
2   St Michael
3   St Andrew
4   Abbot Islip's
5   Chapel of the Pew
6   St John the Baptist
7   St Paul
8   Henry V (over)
9   St Nicholas
10 St Edmund
11 St Benedict
12 St Faith
13 St Gregory
14 Pyx

Henry VII's Chapel

30 m
100 ft

7   8   9

6

5
4   Shrine

10

11

3   2   1   Sanctuary

12

Chapter House

North Transept

South Transept (Poets' Corner)

14

Choir

Great Cloisters

Nave

West Towers 13

Deanery Courtyard

Jerusalem Chamber

College Hall

least four periods – the thirteenth, fourteenth, early sixteenth and eighteenth centuries – the sculpture at Westminster ranks among the best anywhere.

But in other respects the Abbey is not superlative. It is a large church, but not quite as large and lofty as the French cathedrals on which it is modelled. Beautiful though it is, the best French cathedrals surpass it in architectural quality also. Only Henry VII's Chapel has been recognised, almost always, as nonpareil: the antiquarian John Leland called it *miraculum orbis*, a wonder of the world, less than half a century after it was built, and that judgement has been often echoed since. None of its sculptures is among those familiar to everybody, like Michelangelo's *David* or the *Venus de Milo* (a very small class, it is true). Some of its functions are shared with other places: for the last 200 years British kings and queens have been buried at Windsor, and great soldiers and painters mostly in St Paul's Cathedral. St Paul's has also been preferred to the Abbey on some occasions of national celebration or thanksgiving; it has the advantage of being much bigger.

None the less, the Abbey has a quality unlike anywhere else. The Michelin guide to London used to describe it as a realisation of '*la perennité britannique*', and it is indeed a remarkable expression of continuity, but of a continuity which has room for change and evolution. It has been called a shrine of the English or British nation, but it is national in the sense that it represents a community's values and memories; it exhibits little or none of the usual apparatus of patriotic pride. Indeed, it is distinctively international in several ways. Famously, it is the most French in style of all English medieval churches, and later much of its best sculpture was made by foreigners. Among its dead are immigrants and exiles. Its proclaimed ministry has grown steadily wider across the past few centuries, to all the British, to the English-speaking world as a whole, to all Christians and even to people of other faiths.

Westminster Abbey is a *Gesamtkunstwerk*, a coalescence of many arts, in two senses. Visually, its totality includes masterpieces of painting and sculpture, some of them inseparable from the original architectural concept. But it is also a blend of the visual with other arts. To a unique degree, the Abbey is made of words. In this book I shall use reading as a metaphor for architectural appreciation, but we also read the Abbey in a literal sense: there are words everywhere on the monuments that fill it. Pope, Johnson, Scott and Tennyson are among those who have written epitaphs especially for the Abbey. Most of the inscriptions are in English or Latin, but French, Greek, Coptic and Hebrew can also be found; there are fragments of musical scores and even a mathematical equation. Interpreting the Abbey is, in some part, an act of literary criticism; indeed, it may even interpret itself, as in the lines from T. S. Eliot's *Little Gidding* inscribed on his memorial stone in Poets' Corner:

'… the communication
Of the dead is tongued with fire beyond the language of
the living.

The Abbey exists as an idea as well as a building, a nebula of memories, traditions and associations, and so it is made of words in this sense also, that its significance has been formed in part by the writers who have depicted its fabric, moods and activities, among them Shakespeare, Beaumont, Fletcher, Pepys, Addison, Goldsmith, Horace Walpole, Wordsworth, Arnold, Dickens, William Morris, Henry James, Betjeman. Some of these are buried in the Abbey and more are commemorated. From among the authors who have described the building and its atmosphere, I have drawn especially on two nineteenth-century Americans, Washington Irving and Nathaniel Hawthorne. Irving is significant because he wrote with some ambition for a readership which did not know London, while Hawthorne was enthralled and sometimes vexed by the Abbey, returning time and again to test and modify his judgements.

The Abbey is also a house of music, a receptacle filled with sound. Orlando Gibbons and Purcell were among its organists. Much music, including at least two works of undoubted genius, has been written for particular occasions in the Abbey: Purcell's funeral music for Queen Mary, Handel's Coronation Anthems and funeral music for Queen Caroline, Parry's 'I was glad', Walton's 'Crown Imperial', and a great deal more besides. The music of worship is heard here almost every day. For, unlike many of the world's most famous monuments, this is a living entity, still, in however transformed a way, doing the work for which it was built. Any understanding of the Abbey which treats it only as a beautiful shell, without considering what that shell encloses, will be imperfect. But the fabric itself is also living, in the sense that it continues to be adapted and enhanced: a fair amount of new sculpture and stained glass has been installed in the last fifteen years.

This book is partly about a building and partly about its meaning and effect. It does not attempt to tell the history of the medieval monastery (or of Westminster School). But my themes include architecture, sculpture, memory, tradition, sacred space, urban space, ceremony, community, politics and worship; for even in a partial and selective study Westminster Abbey extends into many areas of human experience in a way that few buildings can match. The story begins in the eleventh century with King Edward the Confessor refounding the Abbey and building a great church in the style of Normandy across the Channel. A hundred years on, he was canonised, and thus the Abbey became the shrine of a saint. In the thirteenth century Henry III decided to rebuild, so beginning the construction of what is essentially the church as we know it today. Like the Confessor before him, he looked to the Continent as a model, and the Abbey became a unique mixture of French and English Gothic. Already, though, the story is not purely architectural, as Henry embellishes his church with painting, mosaic, metalwork and sculpture. Already, too, the use and nature of the place were starting to evolve. Henry meant to be buried there himself, but probably without thought for his successors; later kings, however, wanting to lie close to the Confessor's shrine, gradually turned the Abbey into a royal mausoleum.

In the fourteenth and fifteenth centuries Henry III's church was slowly completed, more or less according to the original design. Then, early in the sixteenth century came Henry VII's Chapel, that extraordinary synthesis of northern Gothic and the Italian Renaissance. At the time one might have thought it the first flowering of a new, brilliant and cosmopolitan culture, but in hindsight it was to appear more like an ending, as the Reformation cut English art off from the Continent. Henry VIII abolished the monastery of

1. The nave, looking east. The fourteenth-century nave continues the design of the thirteenth-century eastern limb with only minor modifications. The proportions – very high in relation to width – are French, but the richly ribbed vault, more elaborate than the earlier choir vault, is an English feature.

Westminster, along with every other monastery in the country, and the building lost its primary function. After a while it discovered a new use, as a place of pompous interment. The rich and successful were commemorated by grand monuments, but gradually, by a mixture of design and accident, the idea developed that burial in the Abbey was a national honour – that the criterion for admission should be not prosperity but greatness.

From the sixteenth century onwards, Westminster Abbey also becomes a place to be described, evoked and meditated upon, and we shall hear the voices of its visitors, admiring, criticising, moralising. Melancholy, neglect, gloom and the transience of earthly things were recurrent themes in accounts of the Abbey, until the Victorians made it a busier place and the twentieth century cleaned it. We then move outside, looking at the fabric in relation to the town or city around it and seeing how changes in the urban texture have altered the way in which the building is read. My last chapters turn to the Abbey's public role in the past 200 years. We shall see how in the later nineteenth century it came to be regarded as the proper home for national commemoration, a place of worship that was Anglican, yet communal and inclusive. We might expect the Abbey's significance to have declined in the twentieth century, but on the contrary it grew. The Tomb of the Unknown Warrior has been imitated (though, as I shall suggest, misunderstood) across the world. Coronations became great national and, with the arrival of broadcasting, international events. Are twentieth-century coronations, indeed, an example of 'invented tradition', or should we stress the long continuity of this ritual? Such high ceremonies are political occasions, in a broad sense, but at the end of the twentieth century we also find the Abbey entangled, somewhat surprisingly, in party politics, with each of the last two prime ministers trying to use it to his advantage. And there, more or less, my own account has to end, though one thing at least is sure, that the story of Westminster Abbey itself is not yet concluded, and there will be new chapters to be written in the future.

THE MEDIEVAL CHURCH

The Benedictine Abbey of St Peter, Westminster, first became important when King Edward the Confessor refounded it in the eleventh century. There had been an earlier monastery, but its origins are obscure. One legend attributed its foundation to Sebert, a Saxon king who died early in the seventh century, and the later Middle Ages duly provided a bogus tomb for him close by the authentic kings. An even more fanciful legend pushed the Abbey's beginning back to the second century AD and invented a native British king, Lucius, to establish it.

Even when institutions were genuinely ancient, the medieval imagination often claimed a yet greater antiquity for them. Glastonbury Abbey, for example, was founded in about 700 and a Christian presence there goes back earlier still. But the story was created that the Apostle Philip had paid a visit to Somerset, or that Joseph of Arimathea had come, or even that Christ himself had appeared there before his ascension – hence Blake's question, 'And did those feet in ancient time/Walk upon England's mountains green?' (to which the answer is of course, no). In the case of Westminster, the tale was that a traveller appeared by the river the day before Sebert was to dedicate his church.

Revealing himself to be St Peter, he filled the building with heavenly incense and candlelight. And thus, notionally, the first bishop of Rome inaugurated a long line of prestigious foreigners brought to Westminster to give this English shrine a cosmopolitan éclat.

Edward the Confessor's abbey was indeed cosmopolitan. This was the first church in Saxon England to be built in the style of the Normans across the Channel. It was also England's most ambitious church building, larger indeed than any in Normandy itself. Rising beside the river, a couple of miles out of London, it must have been an astonishing apparition in the mid-eleventh century. Its site was Thorn Ey (Thorn or Bramble Island), surrounded by water, a good place to plant a royal and religious enclave; Canute had already established himself there, earlier in the century, and Edward set about building his own palace. As we shall see, the changing relationship of the Abbey to the Palace of Westminster and to London as a whole was to become part of its history. For the time being, what mattered was that it was near the city but outside it. It was the abbey to the west, the West Minster.

Edward lived to see his church consecrated, on Holy Innocents' Day 1065. A week later, he died, and the next day, 6 January 1066, Harold II became the first king to be crowned there. By the end of that year, England had changed for ever. William the Conqueror had won the Battle of Hastings, Harold was dead and the victor had himself crowned in the Abbey. This coronation, in St Peter's, Westminster, on Christmas Day, emulated Charlemagne, crowned Emperor in St Peter's, Rome, by the Pope on Christmas Day 800. And thus the ritual life of the Abbey, as well as its form, looked beyond England to the Continent. Indeed, it looked beyond France to Rome itself. This too was a presage of its history to come.

Though the Confessor lived to see his abbey consecrated, it may not yet have been complete and construction may have continued after the Conquest. A part of the eleventh-century monastic buildings survives, the oldest vestiges of the Abbey still visible (the present museum, originally the undercroft of the monks' dormitory, dates from this time). But the church as we know it originated in the thirteenth century. In brief and bald summary, the building history is this.

A Lady Chapel was added to the east end of the church in the early thirteenth century. This comparatively small work was to be eclipsed when Henry III decided, around 1240, to replace the Confessor's church with an entirely new structure. The King's master mason, Henry of Reynes, directed the work. Much of the old church was demolished in 1245, and the new work began with the east end and transepts in the following year. About 1253 Henry of Reynes was succeeded as master by John of Gloucester, and John was in turn succeeded about 1260 by Robert of Beverley. John and Robert both continued the original plan with only minor modifications. At the time of Henry III's death, in 1272, the new church extended five bays west of the crossing. For a century after this, the rebuilding ceased, except for some mostly minor works. It was only in the 1370s that the effort to complete Henry III's church was resumed, largely through the vigour of the Abbot, Nicholas Litlyngton, and Simon Langham, a former abbot who had become Archbishop of Canterbury and who made a very large donation. The rest of the Confessor's church was demolished at this time. Richard

II, who came to the throne in 1377, like Henry III a young king with aesthetic-cum-religious ambitions, also extended his patronage to the Abbey. The King's mason, the famous Henry Yevele, was in charge in the 1390s and built the nave arcade. Unusually, the thirteenth-century design was continued with only slight variations. The project advanced slowly throughout the fifteenth century. Early in the sixteenth century Abbot Islip began the western towers, this time in an up-to-date style, but they had reached only roof level when the Reformation brought the monastery to an end. Meanwhile, at the other end of the church, Henry VII had the thirteenth-century Lady Chapel demolished and replaced with a new structure, on which work began in 1503; we know it as Henry VII's Chapel.

After the Reformation, the Abbey's fabric was neglected until the end of the seventeenth century, when Wren was appointed the first surveyor. He began the restoration of the exterior. In the 1740s the church finally got its western towers, designed by Nicholas Hawksmoor and executed after his death by John James. Victorian work on the Abbey was mostly restorative, except for the north transept, where Sir Gilbert Scott and his successor as surveyor, J. L. Pearson, rebuilt the façade, drastically altering the rose window and the porches. In the second half of the twentieth century another major restoration was needed; this was completed in 1995. The interior was also cleaned, transforming its aesthetic effect.

Westminster Abbey is the most French in appearance of all medieval English churches. To see what this means, we need to cast an eye over the history of both French and English Gothic style. And to appreciate the significance of

Gothic itself, it is worth setting it briefly in the broadest context of western architecture.

The architecture of classical Greece was an architecture of the exterior. The Parthenon, built in the fifth century BC, is a culminating example of architecture as a plastic art, the consummate manipulation of outward form. Inside, the colossal gold and ivory statue of the goddess Athena was designed to strike the beholder with awe, but the space in which it stood was hardly more than a dark box to contain it. The Romans, deferential to Greek example and sometimes employing Greek architects, commonly based their temples and colonnades on Hellenic models, but they also made technical advances, which they used in their secular buildings: they invented the arch and they discovered concrete. These innovations enabled them to create much larger interior spaces and to configure them more flexibly. The great basilicas (originally secular halls for meeting or promenading) and bathhouses of imperial Rome show the new possibilities.

Meanwhile, early in the second century AD, a revolution happened: the Emperor Hadrian rebuilt the Pantheon, in the form of a vast circular, domed space. For the first time in the history of Europe, a work of religious architecture was conceived in terms of its interior – that is, in terms of spatial rather than plastic effect. Inside, the Pantheon is a great masterpiece; its outside is comparatively unimportant, indeed in some ways awkward, and originally colonnades hemmed it in to mask the ungainliness. At first, the Pantheon had no successors in the religious sphere, and at Rome the finest architecture of the high empire was secular. But then came the Christians, and for at least a thousand years the supreme efforts of architectural imagination – and the largest resources – would go into church building. And throughout those thousand years it was an architecture of the interior. That is pretty clear in the case of Byzantine churches, where the outsides are comparatively plain and inexpressive. But it is also true of Gothic. Some Gothic exteriors may rival any external architecture whatever, and in particular cases we may judge the exterior finer than the interior, but the fact remains that the demands of interior spatial expression come first. If the interior is so tall and slender that a central tower is impossible, as in the largest French cathedrals, then a central tower is sacrificed. Some flying buttress designs are enormously exciting, but the flying buttress originates as an awkwardness, a structural necessity imposed by the ambitions of the interior. (At Westminster the buttresses are especially powerful on the south side, where they project fifty feet from the nave wall in order to overpass the north cloister walk.) As it happens, the Abbey is unusual among English churches in the degree to which the conception of the interior dominates that of the exterior, but it is a general truth that Gothic architecture is founded on the interior, even though the finest Gothic towers are perhaps the most beautiful ever devised.

Already in the Roman Empire, as soon as they had the freedom and the resources, the Christians began building churches, sometimes of great originality and sometimes on an enormous scale. Since the New Testament declares that on earth we have no abiding home but seek one to come, a new Jerusalem in heaven, we might have expected the Christian triumph to lead to a more modest religious architecture, but on the contrary it erupted into new creativity, inventiveness and ambition. It is in architecture, in fact, that the artistic achievement of late antiquity is highest. Some churches were built, like the Pantheon, on a centralised plan. Most imaginative of all are two churches established by the Emperor Justinian in the sixth century. San Vitale in Ravenna has a semicircular dome supported on an octagon with eight apses, the whole enclosed within a larger octagon – a complexity in the modulation of space that was without precedent. In the church of Hagia Sophia in Constantinople a vast shallow dome floats above two half-domes in a manner that still commands astonishment.

The other type of church plan favoured in late antiquity was the basilica. This is an elongated rectangle, commonly with an apse at the east end, consisting of a central vessel or nave with a lower aisle to each side of it. The central vessel is separated from each aisle by a line of columns (the arcade) and is lighted above the aisle level by a line of windows (the clerestory). In contrast to a polygonal or centrally planned building, the basilica is strongly axial. The march of columns on each side of the nave, and its narrowness in relation to its length, draw the eye firmly towards the altar at the east end. The churches of Santa Maria Maggiore and St Paul outside the Walls in Rome are examples of this type.

And this was the type that set the pattern for the western Middle Ages, with the difference that the ground plan of greater churches was now usually not rectangular but cruciform. The main axis is intersected at right angles by another axis (the transepts), complicating the spatial effect. The area where the two axes intersect, the crossing, interrupts the procession of columns that draw the eye of the spectator in the nave eastwards. Often there is a tower above the crossing, and, in cases where part of that tower is open to the church beneath, the eye is distracted from the eastward view and carried upwards, sometimes to a dizzying height. In greater churches the elevation of the central vessel was commonly not two-stage (arcade below and clerestory above) but three-stage, with a triforium or gallery between arcade and clerestory. (A gallery is a second storey built above the side aisles, with openings on to the central vessel; a triforium is a wall passage or blind arcade at the height of the aisle roof, built into the thickness of the wall. The term 'triforium' is often used for both forms, but it is useful to distinguish between them.)

The cruciform plan is common to cathedrals in the Romanesque or round-arched style and to those of the Gothic period which followed. The Gothic style seems to have sprung suddenly into being with remarkable completeness at St Denis around the middle of the twelfth century. What happened next is as remarkable as anything in the history of architecture. Cathedrals sprouted in northern France one after the other, ever larger and structurally more ambitious. Gothic is an architecture that tends to extremes: in English churches to extreme length, in Spain (in the later Middle Ages) to extreme width and in France to extreme height. In some of the earlier French cathedrals, the designers used a four-stage elevation, with both a gallery and a triforium, to achieve the height they wanted, but they fairly soon found techniques which enabled them to dispense with the gallery. In the supreme works of French High Gothic, the cathedrals of Rheims, Bourges and Amiens, arcades or clerestory or both are immensely tall; the triforium is modest but firmly articulated, a brief counterpoise to the vertical uprush of the slender shafts which rise all the way from ground level to vault.

High Gothic then modulated into a style which French scholars have called Rayonnant ('radiating', from the rose windows, with bar tracery like the spokes of a wheel, which were one of its features). The characteristics of this style are lightness and translucency. Walls are thinned; windows become broader and are no longer deeply splayed. The triforium is no longer separately articulated, but merged into the design of the clerestory, and sometimes itself glazed, so that everything above the level of the arcade seems to liquefy and dissolve into multicoloured transparency. It is an aesthetic of illusion, one that seems to deny the realities of weight and mass. This was the most advanced style when Henry of Reynes set about designing Westminster Abbey.

Gothic crossed the Channel before the end of the twelfth century. The choir of Canterbury Cathedral was rebuilt by the Frenchman William of Sens, a work continued by William the Englishman. At Wells an unknown master designed a nave radically different from the French model. It is not lofty, and the accents of the elevation are horizontal rather than vertical. The piers of the arcade are not cylindrical but shaped as a cluster of thin shafts; the capitals spill out from the columns in tendrils of abstract design but organic expressiveness – a style called stiff-leaf. The stress is upon the rich modulation of mass. Salisbury Cathedral, built in the first half of the thirteenth century, is rather different. The capitals of the arcade are entirely without sculptural ornament (as at Westminster), with an effect of classical restraint. As at Wells, but unlike in High Gothic France, no shafts soar from ground to vault. Compared to French cathedrals, the transepts project much further from the nave and aisles, and the church extends further east from the crossing, even sprouting a second pair of smaller transepts. These features – the long eastward extension and the double transepts – appear in several other English cathedrals. The French cathedral is compacted, gathering its whole force into one immediate and enormous impression. The English cathedral is typically more diffused in effect, more compartmentalised, opening up new rooms or spaces as you walk around it.

France remained the powerhouse of Gothic invention until late in the thirteenth century, when English architecture suddenly became astonishingly innovative. The West Country was especially experimental: the east end of Wells Cathedral is architecture as fugue and as chamber music, the most complex and subtle manipulation of space in the entire history of Gothic, and it is profoundly beautiful. There are varieties of style in this 'Decorated' period; the one that would be most influential in the long run was the curvilinear style, with tracery based on reversed-curve or ogee forms. This manner, exported to the Continent, and there altered and developed, formed the basis of the Flamboyant Gothic of late-medieval France. The English, however, revolutionised their architecture once again in the middle of the fourteenth century: characteristics of the new style were enormous windows and a fondness for rectangular grid patterns applied both to windows and wall surfaces. This Perpendicular style, in contrast with its predecessor, had almost no influence outside England; it was, literally, an insular style. But in England it became so popular that it continued for nearly 200 years, and it is the commonest style in the larger churches surviving from the English Middle Ages.

This is the story into which Westminster Abbey fits, or

fails to fit. Part of its 'foreignness' is a matter of absences. The medieval English were supreme as tower builders, but Westminster Abbey has no medieval towers. The Decorated style is hardly represented at all, except in a small part of the cloister and in the splendid canopies of some of the tombs around the sanctuary. And though most of the nave was built in the Perpendicular period, little of the Perpendicular style itself is found at Westminster before that style's latest, Tudor phase; then it appears in the west front, below the present towers, and in Henry VII's Chapel. But it is not only that the Abbey lacks things which are found in most English cathedrals; it is consciously based on French models and is especially close to Rheims Cathedral. The French characteristic that is most immediately obvious is the ratio of height to width. Westminster Abbey has (by a very small margin) the highest nave vault of any English medieval church, and is easily the highest in relation to its breadth. Not only does the eastern limb terminate in an apse, instead of the square end that was already usual in England, but it has a sequence of chapels radiating from the ambulatory in the French fashion. Nor does the church extend a long way east of the crossing, as the English liked: there are only three bays before the apse begins.

French style carried a prestige which exported it to other countries. The choir of Cologne Cathedral is pure High Gothic, Amiens-on-Rhine; Leon Cathedral is an admirable French Rayonnant church planted on Spanish soil. What happened at Westminster, however, is interestingly different. For one thing, the Abbey does not take a single French model. Hugely important though Rheims is, we shall see that the designer has also absorbed the influence of the latest

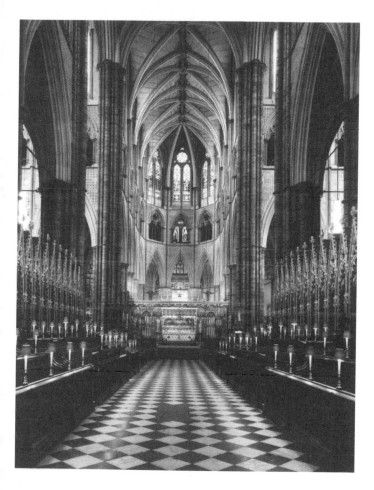

2. The choir and sanctuary. The pillars of the crossing are articulated as a cluster of slender shafts of polished Purbeck marble, emphasising verticality. Behind the altar a screen – built in the fifteenth century, though the western side of it, seen here, is now opulently Victorian – separates the sanctuary from the shrine beyond.

high-tech innovations in Paris at the Sainte-Chapelle and in the transepts of Notre-Dame. The Sainte-Chapelle is more glass than wall, and its huge windows have the bar tracery typical of Rayonnant style. The upper part of the end wall of the south transept of Notre-Dame is all glass, held by slender ribs of stone – a rose window contained within a square, and the whole lower part of that square glazed; the stage below the rose at the triforium level is glazed too. The wall becomes a thin skin, and even that skin is turned into coloured light.

So the Abbey's design draws upon France eclectically, but it is eclectic also in its blend of France and England. For example, Henry of Reynes provided a gallery, with its own windows (mostly invisible inside but prominent on the exterior), instead of the triforium which had become standard in France. The transepts are long, projecting a good way beyond the nave aisles, in the English fashion; each is four bays deep, as against Rheims's two bays. The vault has a ridge rib, an English habit unknown to the French; Henry's successors were to elaborate the vault, adding more ribs in the English manner, as they extended the church westward.

English too is the use of contrasting materials. Northern France is blessed with an abundance of fine limestone (indeed, Caen stone from Normandy was used on a good number of English churches, including Westminster Abbey). The French builders had little incentive, therefore, to experiment with geology as a form of architectural expression. Many parts of England, including the south-east, were not so lucky, and in the event the Abbey's exterior was to suffer greatly from the use of stone that could not stand up to London's sooty air. Where good ashlar was difficult or expensive to obtain, English masons were constrained to use a mixture of stones, and sometimes they made a virtue of necessity. The loveliest example of this is the fourteenth-century interior of Exeter Cathedral. In this West Country church a pleasing chalkstone was used for parts of the walls and vault ribs, but it was not strong enough for the main load-bearing areas. So Purbeck marble, here unpolished and delicately pale grey, was employed for the piers. In other places, a yellowish sandstone was used, and even patches of the rough, purplish local stone, mistaken by some visitors for brick. The warmth and humanity of this interior owe much to the harmonious variety of these materials.

Purbeck marble was a passion among thirteenth-century English masons, independent of necessity. Technically, this Dorset stone is not a marble – that is, a limestone that has been recrystallised under intense heat or pressure – but a limestone that can be polished. It was first used on a large scale in the apse of Canterbury Cathedral, where the gleaming ring of Purbeck piers around the tomb of St Thomas matched the glitter of the mosaic floor and the gold and jewels of his shrine. Purbeck was then extensively employed in Salisbury Cathedral, contributing to its air of cool and slightly aloof elegance. Its lavish use at Westminster is part of the conscious expensiveness of Henry III's showpiece, but it also affects the architectural expression.

Westminster's Purbeck marble is most spectacular at the crossing, where the piers are entirely faced with it all the way from the floor to the springing of the vault. The profile of these piers is more refined than that of their equivalents at Rheims: they are shaped into a cluster of shafts, all very slender, but of varying diameters, gathered in a subtle rhythm. The one horizontal accent is slight and at a comparatively low level: a thin ring of stone at the height of the arcade capitals. So the vertical uprush is checked only for a moment, before soaring onwards much higher still. The marble gleam blends opulence with aspiration. This is one place where Westminster seems for once to trump its French model.

As we look east towards the apse, we see the vaulting ribs received and apparently supported each by a Purbeck shaft, so that the roof seems to be connected to the structure below and held up by it, but with lightness and ease; of course, the idea that these attenuated shafts are taking the weight of the vault is an illusion. If we look west, down the later nave, the effect is a little different. Again we see the vault, now richer and heavier than a French vault would be, seeming to rest on shafts which project from the plane of the wall. But this time only the piers of the main arcade are Purbeck; everything above is of white stone. If we read the elevation of the nave in terms of form, it has a strong verticality, the three stages of the elevation being bound together in each unit of the arcade. But if we read it in terms of material, the piers of the arcade, so distinct in colour and texture, seem to belong to one another more than to the stages above them. Perhaps this is an intriguing ambiguity, perhaps too blunt a contrast.

Who was Henry of Reynes? It seems likely that Reynes is Rheims, and in the past some have supposed that Henry was himself a Frenchman. If this were so, and the English aspects of the design the contribution of his English assistants, the story of the Abbey would be oddly like that of the neo-Gothic Houses of Parliament across the street, where the combination of Barry's overall plan with Pugin's command of decorative detail created a masterpiece that neither of them could have achieved separately. However, it is almost certain

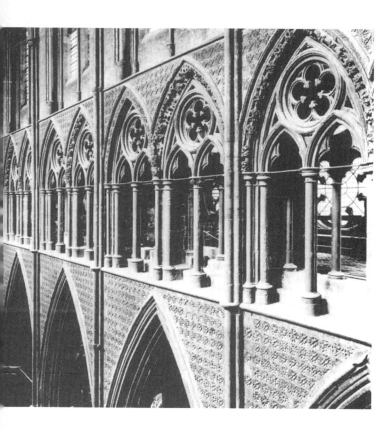

3. This view of the western gallery of the north transept shows how the design cultivates depth in the treatment of wall surface. Flat areas are broken up by diaper patterning. The gallery arcade is doubled, and behind it is a shadowy area lit by windows which are mostly invisible from floor level.

that Henry was English, both because there is too much English in the fundamental conception and because the little we know of his earlier career is enough to indicate that he was not, like William of Sens at Canterbury, a prestigious foreigner imported for a specially prestigious enterprise. His name, then, would be like the Parsee name Calcuttawallah – not the man from Rheims, but the man who had been there. Undoubtedly he knew Rheims well.

The interior of Rheims Cathedral has a distinctive character for which the word is perhaps authority; for all its soaring scale, it has an almost classical serenity and fluidity of form. Westminster Abbey can never have seemed quite like that. Its own character was determined in part by its purpose, and to understand that purpose we need to consider another Henry. Unusually for a great church in the Middle Ages, the Abbey's rebuilding was due not to a community or corporation, but to one man. Henry III's ambition raised it and his money paid for it. Though his reign, from 1216 to 1272, was the longest of the English Middle Ages, Henry was not a capable ruler, but he possessed a personality of some interest. His temperament seems to have been refined, aesthetic and religious, his outlook cosmopolitan and continental. He admired the court culture of Louis IX in Paris and maintained a strong devotion to the papacy. His marriage to Eleanor of Provence brought him into touch with the elegances of Mediterranean civilisation, and he earned unpopularity by the favouritism he showed to her family. He was an extravagant spender and his biggest extravagance was Westminster Abbey.

Why did he rebuild the Abbey? Probably the main reasons were two. He is likely to have had a special devotion to his sainted ancestor the Confessor, who had been canonised in 1161, and to have wished to honour him and be buried in suitable splendour at his side. And he wanted to match the great royal works in France: the coronation church at Rheims and the house of relics in Paris called the Sainte-Chapelle. What he did not intend, pretty certainly, was to found a royal mausoleum for his successors. Since the Conquest, the English kings, unlike the French, had not sought to have themselves buried in one particular church. William the Conqueror was buried at Caen, William II at Winchester, Henry I at Reading, Stephen at Faversham, Henry II and Richard I at Fontevrault and John at Worcester. Henry III surely meant Westminster Abbey to be remembered as his special showpiece, in the way that the Sainte-Chapelle was Louis IX's. The development of the Abbey into a house of many kings was one of the several accidents that mark its history.

The Confessor's shrine and emulation of French royalty are two keys to the appearance of the Abbey's interior. A conspicuous and extraordinary feature of the thirteenth-century work is the amount of flat wall surface covered with small squares of an ornamental patterning called diaper. This too has a French derivation, but nowhere in France is it used across whole areas of interior wall like this. Since the process involves carving a huge area of surface, albeit in a formalised and repetitive pattern, it must have been slow and expensive; indeed, the later diaper work, further west, is larger and coarser, presumably to save time or money or both. Originally there would have been paint and gilding on the diaper. This represents conspicuous expense, a deliberately manifest profusion of treasure. Henry III gave the Confessor a new shrine; but in a sense, the whole of the sanctuary is the saint's shrine, an elaborated outer casing fit to match the glitter of gold and mosaic on the reliquary housing the holy body.

There is, besides, a tension in the eastern limb of the Abbey which differentiates it from the spirit of Rheims. There are two ways of shaping an apse. The wall can curve continuously, as at Canterbury and at St Bartholomew the Great in London; or the apse can be polygonal. The wider the angles of the polygon, the more like it is to a curve. The apse of Rheims is five-sided and not curved; so is the apse of Westminster, but with different effect. The Abbey is slightly higher in relation to its width than Rheims; and the first bay of the apse on each side is canted inwards only very slightly, so that the apse almost looks three-sided. This makes it angular. The arches of the arcade are very sharply pointed, and almost every inch of flat surface is prickling with diaper. Angular, sharp, prickling, this east end is not serene but nervous.

Henry of Reynes's design enjoys and exploits the solidity of walls; it expresses depth and three-dimensionality. The gallery arcade is doubled – there is a second line of piers and arches half hidden behind the first. Behind these is the gallery area itself, which even if it can hardly be seen from below is present partly to the eye and partly to the imagination as a large hollow of shadowy space. Even flat surface is not flat but crinkled by the diaper work into an unceasing undulation: this is wall that draws attention to itself. In these respects the aesthetic of Westminster Abbey is far from the attenuation of Rayonnant style. But elsewhere the Rayonnant influence is strong. Each side of the octagonal chapter house is filled with an immense window of bar tracery, with no area of wall between them. The polygonal chapter house was a distinctively English development, so this is the application of French design to a native form. The ends of the transepts are a blend of another kind – a mixture of Rayonnant skinniness and the articulation of depth.

Let us look at the south transept end (the north transept is similarly conceived, but as we shall see, the south transept had an unusual importance in this building, and besides, the rose window in the north transept was drastically altered in the Victorian restoration). This is a gorgeously rich yet pure composition, in not three but five stages, one above the other, which is a luxuriance in itself. The third and fourth stages are glazed, but the glazing is deeply recessed behind arches; at the fourth stage the paradoxical combination of transparency and the dense, deep clustering of stonework is especially intriguing – it seems to be both a gallery arcade and a line of windows at one and the same time. But the rose window, at the highest stage, is different. This is a membrane of stone ribs and glass, and the design is indeed very close to the transept roses at Notre-Dame. (There are some uncertainties here. The present rose is a reconstruction by Gilbert Scott in the nineteenth century, though it is probably close to the original. The original designer may be either Henry of Reynes or his successor, John of Gloucester, and the Westminster rose may have been built before those at Paris, in which case the master will have known them from plans as yet unexecuted.) As at Notre-Dame, the spandrels are glazed, or, in other words, the whole lower square containing the circle of the rose is glass. The difference is that the vault does not meet the end wall at this

4. The south transept – the first view of the interior for medieval kings and modern tourists alike. Three stages of the spectacular end wall are glazed. In the lower two, the glazing is deeply recessed behind arches, but the rose window above is a skinny membrane of glass and stone, its upper parts vanishing mysteriously above the vault into the roof above.

highest stage but terminates just in front of it, so that the rose appears to float free from the wall, its upper edges vanishing mysteriously into the roof.

Outside, most English cathedrals differed from French as much as they did within. A feature of several is the screen façade – a west end which is a performance in itself, tending to disguise rather than express the design and dimensions of the church behind it. The actual doors are usually insignificant, and in some cases the principal entrance is not on the façade but at the side. The French west front typically represents the form of the interior externally and is dominated by massive, deep porches, projecting forward and richly decorated with sculpture – porches which seem to welcome the spectator to their shelter and draw him into the building. Sometimes the French masters provided the transepts too with magnificent portals, but almost always the west front proclaims itself as the principal entrance.

We do not know what the thirteenth-century masters planned for the west front of the Abbey, but the north transept, nearer to the royal palace, seems to have been meant from the start as the principal and ceremonial entrance. In accord with its unusual importance, it was given a grand triple porch, with statuary to match. But once again, the scheme was not purely French. French were the rose window, the proportions and the prominence given to the porches; but the porches themselves did not stand forward from the façade in the French manner, reaching out to offer the onlooker their embrace. Instead, they were deep hollows punched into the flat surface of the wall. The history of this powerful design was to be melancholy. The sculpture survived the iconoclasm of the Puritans only to be swept away at the start of the eighteenth century, not for religious but for aesthetic reasons: the statues were decayed and modern taste was for tidiness. When Sir Gilbert Scott rebuilt the façade around 1880, he destroyed the porches, replacing them with the present design, a conscientious imitation of thirteenth-century France. And thus it took a robustly patriotic Victorian Englishman to give the north transept, at last, a properly French elevation.

Architecture is, like music, an experience in time, but unlike music buildings allow us to choose the pace and sometimes even the order in which we enjoy them. It makes a difference whether we go round a building fast or slow, whether we move from larger to smaller spaces or the reverse, whether the whole of an interior breaks upon us all at once or is revealed more gradually. Some of the Abbey's literary visitors have been aware of this. Washington Irving begins his 'several hours in rambling about Westminster Abbey' with the tangle of ancillary buildings to the south, walking through low, dark passageways with a subterranean look to them, passing on into the cloister, and only then proceeding into the church itself, so that the force of sudden contrast strikes him amazed at the interior's height and magnitude. Nathaniel Hawthorne enters on the first of his many visits through the north transept, which he supposes to be a side entrance; another time he creeps in through a little door into Poets' Corner, enjoying the sensation of beginning in a small nook within the vast whole.

When we go into a French cathedral through the west door, we are likely to find ourselves enclosed in a dark wooden box. Through the gloom we make out an enamelled label marked '*Poussez*', press and stumble into the church; and then its entire immensity confronts us at one moment, with overwhelming force. Entering, say, Canterbury Cathedral, through the principal porch on the south side, we emerge into an aisle of the nave. At first we get only a partial glimpse of the full height of the building, and not until we advance into the central vessel can we grasp the nave as a whole. At Westminster the latest reorganisation of tourist flow brings visitors in through the north transept. The modern visitor is likely to feel, like Hawthorne, that he has been shown to the side entrance, particularly if he has just gone to the west end and been redirected, but in fact he is taking the same route as a medieval monarch. The first thing that king or pilgrim sees on entering is a 'church', nine bays long, culminating in the end wall of the south transept – that is why this wall has such special importance. Of course, it is an illusion: the apparent church is only the crosspiece at right angles to the main vessel, which has yet to reveal itself.

Standing in the crossing, where nave and transepts meet, we still do not get a clear view of the entire vessel. In terms of architectural form, the nave is the whole length of the church from the west end to the crossing, and the choir is the extension from the crossing eastwards. But liturgically, Westminster Abbey reads differently. The choir, flanked by stalls and closed at the west by a screen called the pulpitum, extends west of the crossing, dividing the nave into two unequal parts. This was a usual pattern in a Benedictine church. As we have seen, though English cathedrals commonly extend a very long way east of the crossing, the Abbey does not. We are standing, therefore, at the focal point of a centralised area, a cross with four arms of roughly equal length. And there is yet another axis intersecting with nave, sanctuary and transepts at the crossing – the vertical axis rising from the floor to the level of the vaults and continuing above them into the tower space. The great French cathedrals commonly have no central tower and the vault of the crossing is at the same height as the rest; the most conspicuous exception is Rouen, a building which shows English influence. Several English cathedrals, on the other hand, have a lantern tower at the crossing – that is, a tower with glazed windows open to the church below. The Abbey's lantern was never built – there is only a stump, itself no older than the eighteenth century, and the painted wooden ceiling is modern, installed after war damage – so we do not look up to a vault at dizzying altitude, with shafts of sun streaming like a benediction from a celestial height, as at Lincoln, Canterbury or York. But the extra lift has an effect, all the same.

In the final reckoning, though, Westminster Abbey is a cruciform church on the conventional plan. As we walk around, we shall adjust our reading of it: when we reach the nave it will be revealed as an axial building, leading the eye eastwards to sanctuary and apse. Essential to the Abbey, however, is its role as a coronation church; but the daily requirements of a monastery and the occasional demands of royal ritual do not necessarily sit well together, and we might guess that the distinctive way in which this abbey church was adjusted to its ceremonial function came about in part fortuitously and in part by design. It seems unsuitable for a coronation church that the choir should be cut off from the nave; it remains true to this day that on a great occasion the bulk of the congregation cannot see what is happening, and before the age of the microphone they could not hear much either.

On the other hand, the crossing is the theatre where the king is crowned, and there is a fitness in its being configured as a focal point. We must imagine the mass of the folk at a medieval coronation packed into the transepts and crowding the galleries above. It was surely for aesthetic or structural reasons that Westminster Abbey was given galleries, but at a coronation they found their use.

The richness with which the church was adorned and furnished also has a royal character. Henry III meant it to be provided with the best painting, carving, bronze and metalwork that the age could produce. One exceptional survival is a thirteenth-century retable (painted panel at the back of an altar), probably made for the high altar itself, which, though terribly damaged, is the finest panel painting of its date north of the Alps. The wall paintings in the south transept, made about 1300, are the grandest of their time remaining in England. Hardly more of the original glass survives than a very few pieces now displayed in the Abbey museum, though there is a fair amount of slightly later glass in the clerestory of the sanctuary. (Canterbury Cathedral is perhaps the only place in England where one can still experience the quality of light which the Abbey would have had at the end of the thirteenth century.) The most ambitious sculptural display in Henry III's church, on the porches of the north transept, has gone entirely; the carved work of the interior is outstanding and pretty varied. Most of the decorative sculpture is grave and refined, but hidden in the choir gallery is a corbel depicting a cheery bloke with a cheeky grin on his face – this has been interpreted as a portrait of one of the builders, or as a representative thirteenth-century cockney. On a larger scale, the elongated figures of Mary and the Angel Gabriel in the chapter house belong in an English tradition and can be compared to the sculptures at Wells Cathedral; in contrast, French influence is strong on the two angels swinging censers on the end wall of the south transept. These famous figures occupy spandrels – that is to say, triangular spaces with the inner side of the triangle concave – difficult areas which the sculptor fills with superlative skill, the wings spreading out at right angles to the long but not attenuated bodies. The problem with angels is how to make them sexless and yet not effeminate, and here it is solved. The French inspiration is most evident in the angels' faces, especially in the face of the right-hand angel, soft, quite broad, slightly smiling, and set off by the richly crisped hair surrounding it. The left-hand angel leans back comfortably against the wall, the other follows his censer slightly forward; both combine grace and serenity with a sense of movement. These figures equal any sculpture made in their time.

Henry III wanted his church to be a treasure house of diverse wonders, but the strangest and perhaps most haunting of these seems not to have come from his initiative. In 1222 Westminster Abbey had gained a rare privilege: it was exempted from the authority of the Bishop of London and the Archbishop of Canterbury and made subject directly to the Pope. Accordingly, when Richard Ware was elected Abbot in 1258, he travelled to Rome to receive his commission. On this or a later journey he returned bringing, in the words of John Flete, a later medieval chronicler, 'stones of porphyry, jasper and marble of Thasos', along with the Italian artists who worked them. Hence that marvel of dull iridescence – like a moth's wing – the Italian mosaic floor of the sanctuary, in a style called Cosmati work, more elaborate

5. Angel with a censer, mid-thirteenth century, on the end wall of the south transept. The style, combining serene grace with a sense of movement, owes much to contemporary work in France, which in turn shows the influence of classical antiquity.

than anything of the kind in Italy itself. This is an exotic wonder in its English setting, yet it also lays claim to a centrality for, like the Conqueror's coronation, it looks beyond France, asserting allegiance to the cultural and spiritual authority of Rome. History has its ironies: now it lies at the spot where the sovereign swears to uphold the Protestant religion by law established.

It drew on another kind of Roman authority too – that of classical antiquity. Formerly it was surrounded by an inscription in brass letters, apparently giving a symbolic explanation of the pavement's abstract design, written in classical Latin metre. However, it slips between two metres, hexameter and the elegiac couplet, behaviour that any classical Roman would have thought barbarous. He might have thought the content even weirder:

> In AD 1212 with 60 less four [i.e. in 1268], King Henry III, the City [i.e. Rome], Odericus [the artist] and the Abbot jointed together these porphyry stones. If the reader should prudently consider everything set down, he will find here the end of the primum mobile. The hedge is of three years; add dogs and horses and men, stags and ravens, eagles, huge sea beasts, the world; whatever follows triples the foregoing years. This spherical globe shows the archetypal macrocosm.

The mindset that produced this may seem to us far more remote than ancient Rome. But the pavement is exotic by any standards: the porphyry will have been quarried in Egypt (though Ware's supply had presumably been brought to Rome in classical times) and the pavement's design draws on the complex pattern-making of the Islamic world. Paris,

6. The mosaic pavement of the sanctuary, as depicted in Ackermann's *The History of the Abbey Church of St Peter's Westminster* (1812). Both the designer, Odericus, and some of the materials were imported from Rome, and the presence of this exotic *tour de force* proclaims Westminster's link to Rome's cultural and spiritual authority.

Rome, even Cairo come to London. Centuries before, Charlemagne had pillaged from Rome sheets of marble to clad the walls of his imperial chapel at Aachen; now, on a smaller scale, Westminster follows his example.

The Italians also made St Edward's shrine and Henry III's tomb-chest, and provided another mosaic floor for the shrine area, so that this holiest, innermost part of the Abbey is also the most foreign. The most popular shrine in England was at Canterbury. There the whole of the cathedral's eastern limb is raised upon a crypt, and the pilgrim had to climb a series of flights of steps before coming into the presence of the saint. It is a dramatic and extended progress through a very long building; there is perhaps no church interior anywhere that uses flights of steps as excitingly as this. Westminster could not quite match such drama; even so, the shrine area is a little higher than the sanctuary, which is in turn a little higher than the nave. But unlike at Canterbury, the floor level of the aisles remains at the same level as the nave, so that the shrine area is some six feet above the ambulatory and hidden from it. Entrance to the shrine area is narrow and awkward, and seemingly must always have been so. Henry's tomb is superb, purely Italian and curiously timeless. With its slabs of antique porphyry, more or less classical pilasters and even a classical pediment on one side, it looks back to ancient Rome, and yet is also a harbinger of a Renaissance that would not reach England for another two and a half centuries. The calm expanses of the porphyry set off the intricate detail of the gilded mosaic work. On the shrine side, the tomb has had its gilding picked away, but high above the ambulatory its aloof and alien glitter remains.

On top of the tomb lies the gilt-bronze effigy of the King,

7. The tomb of Henry III, another work by the Italian masters known as the Cosmati. The slab of Egyptian porphyry on the upper part, the colour of clotted blood, was brought from Rome. Below, a pediment and pilasters bring a memory of classical antiquity to the medieval north. The gilt-bronze effigy of the king is by the Englishman, William Torel.

by the English goldsmith William Torel, mild, vulnerable yet somehow regal. The tomb-chest is so high that the effigy is almost invisible from the ambulatory, and even from the shrine is not easily seen. There is something almost Egyptian in a funerary art which creates such costly beauty and seems hardly to care if anyone can look upon it. Edward I, Henry's son, who had commissioned Torel to make his father's image, called upon him again for the effigy of his wife, Eleanor of Castile. This is even finer, one of the loveliest of all medieval tombs, and this time it can be easily seen from the shrine area, but it is concealed from the ambulatory by a magnificent iron grille. This perhaps marks the beginning of a process which makes the shrine area more private and turned inward, as it acquires its second function as a royal burial chapel.

Edward I was in turn buried here, in a plain dark marble tomb without an effigy. Queen Philippa was commemorated in alabaster, and her husband, Edward III, in gilt bronze. His image has a stiff, archaic nobility, but it is hard to credit that it is almost a century later than Torel's work; one would have guessed that the dates were the other way round. After the death of his queen, Anne of Bohemia, Richard II had a tomb made for them both, in his own lifetime. That was as well, since Henry IV was soon to depose him. Henry IV himself may not have wished his own tomb to stand close to the man whom he had overthrown; at all events, he lies in Canterbury Cathedral, the only king buried there. But Henry V, his son, wished to join his predecessors in the horseshoe around the shrine at Westminster; he also required his own chantry chapel, where masses could be said for the repose of his soul. And thus for the first time a problem arose that was to return in the Abbey's history: it was running out of space.

8. When Edward I placed the tomb of his wife, Eleanor of Castile, next to that of his father, Henry III, he began the process that would turn the shrine area into a royal mausoleum. William Torel's effigy of Queen Eleanor combines ideality and naturalism.

The solution was extraordinary: to build a kind of mezzanine within the eastern ambulatory. A bridge links the east end of the shrine to what is now the entrance to Henry VII's Chapel. The raised floor of the shrine area was extended eastward to make a platform for the King's tomb, and the eastern piers of the apse were encased in a skein of stone enclosing staircases leading to an upper chapel overlooking the shrine – a chapel within a chapel within a church. Meanwhile, as the shrine area was pressed upon by Henry V's chantry chapel from the east, to the west it was totally separated from the choir and sanctuary by the construction of a massive stone reredos. This completed the conversion of the shrine area into an apparently private space, rather like those chapels in some parish churches which noble families reserved for their monuments. From the later fifteenth century the tiny tombs of two princesses who died in early childhood, stuffed with touching clumsiness in front of a couple of pillars, add a domestic note. Yet this cannot quite have been a place of private memory, for it remained, after all, a saint's shrine. At the Reformation the shrine itself was mutilated, and the present wooden superstructure dates from the 1550s – a temporary expedient ordered by Mary I during her short-lived Catholic restoration. Since then the shrine area has hardly changed at all. It now has an altar once again, with a booklet of prayers upon it to guide the modern pilgrim's devotions.

This is an astonishing place, impossible to represent in a photograph and not much easier to describe in words. The ring of gilded kings and queens is especially rare and strange (there is nothing quite like it anywhere else in Europe); it is hard to believe that one is in England, let alone a couple of hundred yards from the jabber of Parliament and the blankness of Victoria Street. Yet despite their costliness, these royal images do not seem haughty or ostentatious but humane. Even Henry III's effigy was described at the time as his likeness, though it must have been an idealised likeness, and the later figures increasingly resemble portraits: Richard II, for example, clearly has the same face on his tomb as in the painting of him at the west end of the nave. In later times many visitors to the Abbey were to contrast the medieval tombs with the pride and pomp of more recent monuments. Many, too, especially in the centuries of the Abbey's neglect, were struck by the contrast between the bustle of London outside and the stillness within. But like a Russian doll, the church's interior repeats that pattern. As the Abbey is an oasis of sanctity within London, so the shrine area is a still point inside the busy life of the Abbey, where the shuffle of invisible tourists around the ambulatory below is muffled and softened to a seemingly distant murmur. Like the womb, this place is secret and sacred, intimate and exotic; it is the habitation of historic memory, yet mysterious. But it is not, as Henry VII's Chapel is, an independent room or building. Standing in the shrine one is still within the church, looking out past Gothic pillars at the golden gleam of Elizabethan worldliness in the monuments of the ambulatory chapels or across Poets' Corner to the baroque vitality of the Duke of Argyll's tomb. It is among the enchantments of this space that it is apart and yet not separate. But its beauty, power and holiness are not things that anyone could have designed; they have evolved, like the British constitution, through the accidents of time and chance. In that at least, the shrine is not so foreign after all.

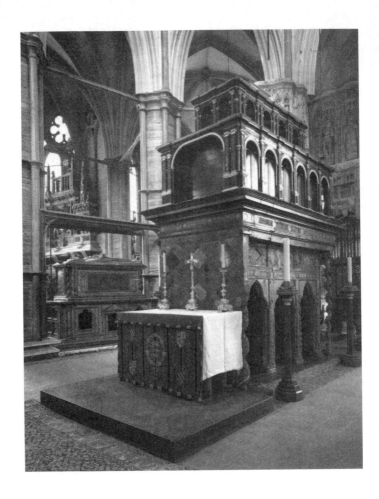

9. The thirteenth-century shrine of Edward the Confessor, king and saint, was designed by Pietro Oderisi, either the master of the sanctuary pavement or his son. Originally it was crowned by a golden and bejewelled 'feretory' or bier. This was destroyed at the Reformation. The present wooden superstructure dates from Mary I's short-lived Catholic restoration in the 1550s.

....

2

HENRY VII'S CHAPEL

Given the importance that Henry III attached to Westminster Abbey and the amount of money he threw at it, we may feel surprised that progress was not faster. It is curious, too, that neither the Abbey's own wealth nor the patronage of the kings who chose to be buried there pushed forward the completion of the nave more vigorously. That completion followed the earlier design with only minor variations (most obviously, the diaper work was abandoned) and no radical innovations until the Tudor age, when Abbot Islip began to build the western towers and Henry VII rebuilt the Lady Chapel. Everyone is impressed by Henry VII's Chapel, but it may well strike us as more worldly, more secular, than the rest of the church. Like so much in the Abbey's history, this has come about partly by design, partly by accident.

Henry VII's is the last in conception of four great royal chapels of the Perpendicular age, the others being Eton College Chapel, King's College Chapel, Cambridge, and St George's Chapel, Windsor. King's College Chapel, begun in 1446, is a rectangular box, long and high, a simple form articulated with consummate refinement. So perfect does the whole appear that it is hard to believe that the fan vault was not part of the original plan, but it is in fact a later design, by

John Wastell, and from the same Tudor period as the chapel at Westminster. Much of the decoration at King's is Tudor also. Yet these two masterpieces, using the same Perpendicular vocabulary and sharing a taste for sumptuousness and technical virtuosity, differ radically in their spatial sense. Together they show the expressive range of a style which is sometimes thought to lack variety.

Henry VII's Chapel acknowledges the design of the thirteenth-century Abbey, even as it contrasts with it. Though intended as a Lady Chapel, it is planned as a whole church in itself, with nave and aisles, a great west window and even a kind of chancel arch. The polygonal apse echoes the form of the main building, even to the extent of having five radiating chapels. So, unlike King's, this is a vessel of complex shape; but it is even more complex than this basic description suggests.

Let us look at the outside first. At the ground level no line is allowed to continue straight for more than a few feet: the aisle wall is broken up into a ceaseless pattern of advance and recession. Each of the buttresses is elaborated into a polygonal tower, rising high above the aisles and capped with a cupola. Between the buttresses is a line of square-topped bay windows, curved except at the apse, where like folded paper they are crinkled into multiple angular projections. So emphatic are the buttresses that we can read the aisles as an alternation between solid towers and walls that are almost all glass; yet buttresses and windows are assimilated to each other by a remorseless grid of mullions and horizontals, so that we also read windows and panelled wall as a single tight but continuously undulant surface. This style of fenestration has a secular air; there are parallels in one or two grand

10. The interior of Henry VII's Chapel. The plan echoes the Abbey as a whole: nave, chancel arch and apse with radiating chapels. The roof combines fan vault and pendant vault, with the illusion that the pendants, actually anchored in the transverse arches, hang from the fans.

houses of the period, but no other church has anything like it. The cupolas are topped with gilded weather vanes, restored in the last quarter-century after long absence, with a festiveness that calls to mind a pleasure boat under sail. Christopher Wren, too, writing in his survey of the Abbey about the chapel's 'flutter of arch buttresses', seems to catch the spirit of almost nautical gaiety. Seen from outside the building is obviously a church, but a church conceived in a rather secular spirit.

Now let us walk inside. The interior seems a superlatively harmonious whole; yet recent research has suggested that the upper parts represent a change of plan. If so, the crowning perfection, as at Cambridge, was not part of the original scheme. The building's lively and festive spirit, however, is quite unlike King's. The east end is as transparent and spatially vivid as we would expect from the exterior view. There is no flat wall surface anywhere: every inch of wall is shaped into moulding, canopy, pedestal or niche, animated by the carved figures of saints, about a hundred in all. Several sculptors must have been employed. Some of the figures are distinguished by a tall, calm fluidity; another master shows a keen sense of individual character and a fondness for hats flamboyant enough for Ascot (on men, however). But it is the roof that dominates – the most spectacular vault in existence. Washington Irving's eloquence is worth quoting:

> *The very walls are wrought into universal ornament, encrusted with tracery, and scooped into niches, crowded with the statues of saints and martyrs. Stone seems, by the cunning labour of the chisel, to have been robbed of its weight and density, suspended*

*aloft, as if by magic, and the fretted roof achieved with the
wonderful minuteness and airy security of a cobweb.*

But of course it is not magic; so how is it done?

In the Perpendicular period English masons invented two new forms of vault. The first is the fan vault, devised in the late fourteenth century but most familiar to many from the roof of King's College Chapel, Cambridge. This is, however, an untypical fan vault in that it also uses transverse arches – that is, structural ribs crossing the entire roof at right angles to the walls. The other invention is the pendant vault. In the Divinity School, Oxford, William Orchard devised massive transverse arches which are interpenetrated by stone pendants, apparently hung from the roof, carved into canopies with statuettes inside them. At Christ Church Cathedral, Oxford, a little later, the designer, probably Orchard again, created a subtler variant on this theme. This time the central parts of the transverse arches vanish beneath a skein of stone ribs, so that the means by which the pendants are supported seem even more mysterious. The pendants themselves are now longer and more delicate, hollowed out into semi-transparent lanterns.

The roof of Henry VII's Chapel combines these types: it is both a fan vault and a pendant vault, with transverse arches, and part of its ebullience comes from this brilliant synthesis of forms. The man of genius who designed it was almost certainly William Vertue. At the apsidal east end the fans flower into a ring of almost complete circles, frilly-edged, with pendants descending from them, floating like a school of fine-filamented jellyfish seen from below. They enclose the star-like form of a concave octagon, one corner of which is cut off by the broad transverse arch separating the chapel's nave from its apse – a tiny flaw in this marvellous composition, invisible except at the east end. In the nave the fans expand further outwards into segments which intersect, as at King's. In structural terms, the pendants are the extensions of voussoirs – that is, of the wedge-shaped stones that make up the transverse arch. So the impression of stalactites hanging from the roof of a fairy cavern is not entirely untrue to the structural reality: each pendant is a monolith, rooted in the vault above, even if it does not literally grow out of it. This is none the less an architecture of illusion, partly because the pendants seem to hang not from the arches but from the fans, gathered from above like a drop of water about to fall, and partly because the vertical hang of the pendants appears quite unconnected to the angled position of the transverse arch. And despite the stalactite effect, the elaborated design of the pendants themselves discourages us from reading them as the monoliths that they actually are, and this too contributes to the air of miracle.

But it is no illusion that this roof is a prodigious work. A vault was normally made of ribs with infill between them. Exceptionally, this vault is made entirely from blocks of cut and moulded stone. This is a very difficult technique, but it makes possible that mixture of depth of cutting and extreme delicacy of detail which gives the roof its appearance of coralline encrustation. The organic metaphor is hard to resist, but it does not do full justice to the work, for part of its mastery lies in its fusion of utmost elaboration with a strong and lucid overall design. 'We have lost now, I think,' wrote Hawthorne on first seeing the chapel, 'this faculty of combining breadth of effect with minuteness of finish.'

Gaiety and bravura were built into the chapel from the start, but its present air of half-secular magnificence is in part accidental. Originally the windows, now mostly clear, were filled with stained glass, smashed by Puritan iconoclasts after the Civil War; to recover the effect, one must go to King's, where the contemporary glass has survived. Henry VII actually intended his chapel to be a place of especial sanctity, for it was to double as a Lady Chapel and the shrine of a second royal saint. His hope was to persuade the Pope to canonise King Henry VI; in the event, the pontiff's price proved too steep. Had the plan come off, Henry VII would have matched Henry III as a shrine builder, and indeed the floor of his chapel is raised to the same level as that of the Confessor's shrine, so that there should be no inferiority. Instead, the King's own tomb became the centrepiece, a display of earthly pomp so potent that in the public mind the Lady Chapel turned into Henry VII's Chapel, as though it had been built from the start as his mausoleum. (Recently the Dean and Chapter have tried to bring the name Lady Chapel back into use; they are unlikely to succeed.)

Henry VII also looked to rival his earlier namesake in making his chapel a cosmopolitan assemblage of the various arts. The glass was commissioned from Bernard Flower, a Netherlander; the screen around the royal tomb was made by Thomas Dutchman, whose name indicates an origin in Germany or the Low Countries; and one or more of the sculptors may have been Netherlandish too. The most spectacular import was the Italian Pietro Torrigiani, who made the tomb of Henry VII and his queen, Elizabeth of York, commissioned by their son Henry VIII, as well as the tomb of Henry VII's mother, Lady Margaret Beaufort, in the south aisle. These masterpieces need no addition to the praise that they have always been given, though a special mention might be made of the four young angels who sit at the corners of the King and Queen's tomb-chest, displaying the Florentine Renaissance at its purest and most poignant. And thus Perpendicular Gothic, a style rooted in the medieval past, here meets the art of the future, but without discomfort, and on terms of equality. Any visitor to the chapel in (let us say) 1520, at the time of Cardinal Wolsey's ascendancy, observing a native architecture of supreme self-assurance commingled with an openness to Italy and the Renaissance, might confidently have said that England was on the brink of developing a visual culture of especial brilliance. He would have been entirely mistaken.

3

RENAISSANCE AND REFORMATION

The ripest fruits of architectural expression often come just before the fall. The most swaggering part of the Hofburg, the imperial palace complex in Vienna, was finished in 1912, half a dozen years before the Habsburg empire collapsed; the vast imperial capital of New Delhi was built just as the British Raj was about to vanish for ever. At Westminster, while Henry VII put up his chapel at the east end, with instructions for 10,000 masses to be said there for his soul and prayers to be offered for him 'as long as the world shall endure', Abbot Islip was building the west end, and finally constructing its towers (though they got no further than the roofline). He too made careful arrangements for the next life, the only abbot to equip himself with his own chantry chapel inside the church. His obsequies, in 1532, are described and illustrated in a remarkable document known as the Islip Roll, which provides the earliest pictures of the Abbey's interior. In these images of medieval pomp and piety, it is as though the Reformation were a thousand years away. But even as Islip lay dying, the old order was yielding. It was in the chapter house at Westminster that the Commons passed the Acts of Supremacy and Submission, requiring the clergy to acknowledge the king's command over the Church. Meanwhile,

Henry VIII was dissolving the monasteries, abolishing the religious houses and turning out every monk, nun and friar in his kingdom. The new abbot, William Boston, was not one of the Westminster monks, as was customary, but was brought in from outside, presumably to do the bidding of the King and his minister Thomas Cromwell. In 1536 the golden feretory or bier was stripped from the Confessor's shrine, though the saint's royal status enabled the main structure of the shrine to survive, gaunt and battered. Four years later, the Abbot and his monks gathered in the chapter house to surrender their monastery to the King, and the abbey of Westminster was no more.

For a brief time the building acquired a new use. Henry founded six new dioceses, converting the same number of abbey churches to serve as their cathedrals; Westminster was one of these, which is why there are both a City of London and a City of Westminster to this day. He established a Dean and Chapter to govern the cathedral, attaching to them a school and choristers. Only ten years later, under Edward VI, the new diocese was abolished, though for a short period the building shared the status of cathedral with St Paul's. In 1556 Mary I, as part of her Catholic restoration, dissolved the Dean and Chapter and re-established the monastery. This was the shortest dispensation of all: Mary died two years later, and in 1559 Queen Elizabeth again dissolved all religious houses. At Westminster she brought back what were more or less her father's arrangements: a Dean and Chapter, and a school attached to them. Westminster School regards her as its foundress. The story of the school, which became one of the most fashionable in the country, is outside this book's scope, except for two matters. First, despite a period of violent change, there was a continuity: Westminster Abbey has always been and remains, among other things, a place of study and education. Second, the growth of a large school on the site brought about one of those collisions of the sacred and the everyday that recur in the Abbey's history: from now on schoolboy rowdiness and even vandalism will both batter and humanise the life and fabric of the place. There had been a school on the Abbey site from the fourteenth century, and surely the pupils then were not always quiet, but they were perhaps better disciplined than their successors in later times. In the eighteenth century Westminster boys were to deface the Coronation Chair, frighten off Horace Walpole and persecute William Blake; as late as Queen Victoria's time they disturbed the consecration of four colonial bishops with a bare-knuckle fight in the cloister.

The middle part of the sixteenth century was the most turbulent part of the Abbey's history and for that reason the most barren artistically. Elizabeth's collegiate foundation had saved the building, but it remained a large church on the edge of London with not quite enough to justify its size. It is, after all, rather big for a school chapel. With the cult of saints abolished, the chapels radiating from the eastern limb were no longer wanted for worship, but for these at least a new use was soon found, as a repository for funerary monuments. These late-Elizabethan tombs vary in quality, but none matches the masterpieces of the previous centuries; some of them, however, are much bigger. No king has so tall or gaudy a memorial, for example, as Anne, Duchess of Somerset. Most megalomaniac of all is the tomb of the courtier and administrator Lord Hunsdon, the highest monument in the Abbey. This unabashed celebration of worldliness is without human imagery or religious content. It is not crude or inept; its spectacular display of heraldry, gilding and many-coloured marbles is, of its kind, highly accomplished; but despite the parade of classical columns, trophies and obelisks, it is unmistakably provincial. This is the product of a culture distant from the European mainstream.

There is indeed an extraordinary disjunction between the Elizabethans' visual and literary culture: their art so quaint and awkward, their poetry so great. But if we go to St Helen Bishopgate, in the City of London, we can find a tomb more sophisticated than anything of its date in the Abbey. This is the monument to Sir Thomas Gresham, merchant and diplomat, who had lived in continental Europe. It too lacks figurative imagery, but achieves an impressive fusion of antique restraint with a degree of controlled Renaissance swagger. It reminds us that in the later sixteenth century the Abbey was just one among London's churches and not at the heart of the urban fabric; its particular advantage as a site for funerary monuments was that, for the time being, it had plenty of room. For centuries its tombs had equalled or out-classed the best in England, but now this could no longer be securely claimed. Royal tombs are a special case, but they did not begin to be made again until the seventeenth century. In the next few generations the history of the Abbey's sculpture will be one of recovery, of finding again those connections with the heart of Europe which the building had displayed in the reigns of Henry III and Henry VII.

As it happens, the native sculptors of the early seventeenth century are under-represented in the Abbey. Epiphanius Evesham has been called the best among the English sculptors of his day, a distinction akin to being the

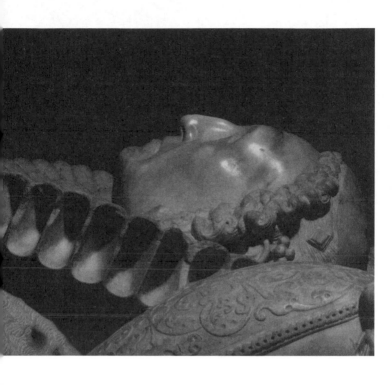

11. The royal tombs of the early seventeenth century return an international, cosmopolitan note to the Abbey. Maximilian Colt's recumbent effigy of Elizabeth I (died 1603) gives a vivid sense of her personality.

best British player at Wimbledon. Some attribute to him the touching relief commemorating Juliana Crewe, who is shown dying in bed with her family around her, but its gentle domesticity does not seem quite strong or individual enough to be his work. Nicholas Stone, half a generation younger, did make several of the Abbey's monuments, most notably perhaps his seated statue of Francis Holles. Modelled on a figure from Michelangelo's Medici Chapel in Florence, it brings a shadow of the Italian Renaissance back within the Abbey's walls. Stone's Westminster monuments have been diversely judged (somewhat unexpectedly, Pevsner was lavish in praise), but on any account his finest work is elsewhere. The more glamorous commissions tended to go to foreigners: Colt and Cure from the Low Countries, Le Sueur from France, Fanelli from Italy.

In 1603 James I succeeded Queen Elizabeth, the woman who had ordered the beheading of his mother, Mary Queen of Scots. He had both of them handsomely commemorated. Elizabeth is in the north aisle of Henry VII's Chapel; the effigy, by Maximilian Colt, captures her character and force of personality. Mary lies in the corresponding position on the south side; her tomb was begun by Cornelius Cure, but the beautiful effigy is probably by his English-born son William. Protest at her fate is confined to the Latin verses on her sarcophagus. The symmetry between these two monuments has always seemed expressive: Washington Irving noted with satisfaction, but not certainly with accuracy, 'The walls of Elizabeth's sepulchre continually echo with the sighs of sympathy heaved at the grave of her rival.' In any case, the symmetry might be interpreted more irenically – the two women, who never met in life, united and equal in death. In a union of another kind, Catholic Mary I shares the tomb of Elizabeth, her Protestant half-sister; a modern inscription on the floor asks us to remember all those, of different convictions, who died for their beliefs at the Reformation. Elizabeth and the Queen of Scots, Elizabeth and Bloody Mary – the Abbey was beginning its work as (in Macaulay's words) a 'temple of reconciliation'.

James I also brought the touch of private domesticity into Henry VII's Chapel, with monuments to two of his daughters who died as infants. These were not the first royal infants to lie in the Abbey – we have seen a couple of small tombs by the Confessor's shrine – but they had not been portrayed before. The effigy of Princess Mary is a surprisingly gauche piece, the sort of thing one might find in the parish church of a market town anywhere in England, but Princess Sophia, who died only a few days after birth, is more sweetly remembered. The inscription is worth reading:

Sophia rosula regia praepropero fato decerpta et Iacobo magnae Britanniae Franciae et Hiberniae regi, Annaeque, Reginae, parentibus erepta, ut in Christi rosario reflorescat, hic sita est …

(Sophia, royal rosebud, plucked by a premature fate and snatched from her parents, James, King of Great Britain, France and Ireland, and Queen Anne, to bloom again in Christ's rose garden, lies here…)

'*Rosula*', little rose or rosebud, is a diminutive form in Latin, with a colloquial character: it gives an intimate, family flavour to the baby's commemoration. The charm of the inscription lies in the way that the pretty conceit of the rosebud is interrupted by the sonorous recital of formal, royal titles (including the claim to rule over France, which the British monarchs kept up for some centuries after it had become absurd), only to be picked up again in words which link infancy on earth to life in heaven.

For the tomb to have its full effect, the words and the object should be taken together. The tomb is one of the best remembered in the Abbey, for it is in the form of an alabaster cradle, realistically carved and coloured (a 'questionable conceit', mutters Pevsner, oddly crusty), with the baby's bonneted head peeping out from her bedding – like any other infant, except for the richness of the ornament and the royal hatchment by her feet. Inscription and sculpture unite in expressing a coalescence of the unique and the universal, the royal and the tenderly ordinary.

We have seen that Henry VII had intended to build a shrine to rival the one made by Henry III. That did not happen; but James I effectively turned Henry VII's Chapel into a second royal burying ground, matching the sequence round the Confessor (though astonishingly neither James nor any of the monarchs buried there after him has any monument whatever). Henry VII's Chapel had become distinctively and exclusively royal. The tomb of George Villiers, Duke of Buckingham (1592–1628), is hardly an exception, since he owes his place in the chapel to his status as an assassinated royal favourite. The Duke and Duchess lie very grand and formal in bronze (by Le Sueur); above, their children, carved in stone by another hand, kneel in modest prayer. The contrast of styles and materials brings public and domestic together within a single monument. Not until the early eighteenth century did an unrelated Buckingham – John Sheffield, first Duke of the second creation – decisively break the royal monopoly on burial in the chapel, smashing his huge monument into the wall surface, obliterating three of the original statues and much ornament besides, and inscribing the superbly haughty and defiant declaration, '*Pro Rege saepe Pro Republica semper*' (For King, often; for Country, always). But even he was an exception: the fact that his widow was the bastard daughter of James II may have made a difference, and certainly the other major baroque monuments went elsewhere. Meanwhile, the rest of the Abbey remained private and ordinary, in the sense that people of no great distinction or grandeur could still be buried and commemorated there. The family of the Dukes of Northumberland retain even now the right to lie in the Abbey – not exactly the common folk, but none the less a survival from the time when, as far as burial went, Westminster Abbey was one London church among many.

🏛

The Abbey's history was almost as disturbed in the middle of the seventeenth century as it had been a hundred years earlier. The battle within the Church of England was played out in microcosm at Westminster in the contention between the Protestant John Williams, Dean from 1620 to 1644, and one of his canons, the high churchman William Laud. Laud was to become Archbishop of Canterbury and Williams successively Bishop of Lincoln and Archbishop of York, continuing as Dean for most of that time. Both men are part of English history, triumphing and suffering in the violent upheavals of their age; at one point the two contending arch-bishops were imprisoned in the Tower of London at the same time. The Civil War did worse damage to the Abbey than the Reformation: altars, stained glass, the organ and the crown jewels were smashed or destroyed. Dean and Chapter were swept away once more and a Presbyterian order imposed. One or two queer continuities remained: Cromwell had himself installed as Lord Protector upon the Coronation Chair and the Stone of Scone, though in Westminster Hall, not the Abbey; and he was buried among the kings, in Henry VII's Chapel. At the Restoration, in 1660, the Anglican order returned. One memory of the interregnum survives. For five years in the 1640s the Presbyterian Assembly of Divines met in the Abbey, in Henry VII's Chapel – beneath the most gorgeous roof in Christendom, with a hundred Catholic saints looking down upon them – and in the Jerusalem Chamber (the hall attached to the west end of the church, now part of the Deanery), and there they drew up the Longer and Shorter Catechisms and the Westminster Confession. And thus a quirk of history has given the Abbey's name to various Presbyterian foundations, among them Westminster College, Missouri, where Churchill was to deliver his 'iron curtain' speech.

Through all these vicissitudes, and on until the beginning of the Victorian age, the fabric was neglected. By the end of the seventeenth century, the need for repair was becoming clear, and the Dean and Chapter appointed Sir Christopher Wren as surveyor. He and his successor, William Dickinson, carried out the first major restoration of the exterior. That kept the church standing; but the interior, or at least its eastern part, was virtually abandoned to indifference and petty vandalism. It is strange that royal and historic memories were treated with such profound unconcern. Schoolboys fought in the aisle with Richard II's jawbone, until one of them stole it. Most amazing of all is the fate of Henry V's queen, Catherine of Valois. She had been laid in the Lady Chapel (no room for her beside her husband), disinterred during Henry VII's rebuilding and never reburied. The curious could pay to see her, and Pepys for one, a man who found the Abbey a good place for assignations, enjoyed here a more macabre flirtation: 'And here we did see, by particular favour, Queen Katherine of Valois, and had her upper part of her body in my hands. And I did kiss her mouth, reflecting upon it that I did kiss a Queen, and that this was my birthday, 36 year old, that I did first kiss a Queen.' Eighteenth-century schoolboys carved their names on tombs and on the Coronation Chair, scandalising later visitors. The boy who recorded that he had spent the night sleeping in the chair must have occupied it for longer than any king. Washington Irving exclaimed at the 'shocking levity of some natures' and the sight of royal monuments 'covered with ribaldry and insult'. Yet a part of him is gratified by these desecrations, enhancing as they do his evocation, like Shelley's *Ozymandias*, of the passing vanity of earthly glory. Hawthorne, more wryly, decided that his compatriots would have made a better job of the Coronation Chair, 'quite covered… with initials cut into it with pocket-knives, just as the Yankees would do it; only it is not whittled away, as would have been its fate in our hands'.

We are bound to wonder if this indifference was due to a change of taste. Was it disdain for the art of the Middle Ages which led to such neglect? The answer to this question is not

12. The exterior of Henry VII's Chapel. A firm stone grid binds together the complex, undulating forms of the lower windows and the towers between them. John Evelyn deplored the chapel's 'sharp angles ... lace and other cutwork and crinkle-crankle', but Wren allowed that it was 'nice embroidered work', with a 'flutter of arch buttresses'.

simple. Certainly John Evelyn, one of the chief architectural authorities of his day, was forthright. After explaining that Gothic architecture was a barbarian import, derived from Goths and Vandals to the north, and Moors and Arabs to the south and east, he continued by declaring that he could rely on the agreement of 'any man of judgement and that has the least taste of order and magnificence'. No such person could be in any doubt

if after he has looked a while upon King Henry the VIIth's Chapel at Westminster; gazed on its sharp angles, jetties, narrow lights, lame statues, lace and other cutwork and crinkle-crankle; and shall then turn his eyes on the Banqueting House, built at Whitehall by Inigo Jones after the ancient manner, or on what his Majesty's present Surveyor Sir Christopher Wren has lately advanced at St. Paul's; and consider what a glorious object the designed cupola, portico, colonnades and other (yet unfinished) parts will then present to the beholder...

Finally, Evelyn catalogues the greater English churches, with the Abbey heading the roll call of inadequacy: 'Witness... Westminster, Canterbury, Salisbury...' (the list continues for some time) 'and compare them (almost numberless as they are) with one St. Peter's at Rome only.'

Wren himself, reporting on the Abbey after his appointment as surveyor, struck a similar note: 'The Goths and Vandals, having demolished the Greek and Roman architecture, introduced... a certain fantastical and licentious manner of building which we have since called modern or Gothic – of the greatest industry and expressive carving, full of fret and lamentable imagery, sparing neither pains nor cost...' 'Full of fret and lamentable imagery' is a glorious phrase, worthy of a man who understood the ambiguities of baroque form. 'Fret' of course means fretwork, interlaced patterning, but in this context it also suggests the unrelated 'fret' in the sense of irritable fuss. 'Lamentable' works in the opposite direction, from the metaphorical to the literal: the primary meaning is presumably 'poor in quality', but we remember that the Abbey is indeed replete with the iconography of mourning. 'Pains' and 'cost' pick up and continue the ambivalent note.

Undoubtedly Gothic architecture suffered a loss of esteem in the early modern period, but this can easily be exaggerated, at least where England is concerned. The English have never wholly lost their affection for Gothic and have put up major buildings in the style in every century from the twelfth to the twentieth. Liverpool Cathedral, larger than any medieval church in northern Europe, was begun only in 1904, while the British diaspora across the seas has ensured that the city with the highest number of very big Gothic churches is not Paris, Rouen or London, but New York. Wren himself was prepared to design in Gothic where it harmonised with older buildings, as at Christ Church, Oxford, or in his unexecuted plans for the towers of Westminster Abbey; it is interesting to contrast the flexibility of this seventeenth-century modernist with some of his twentieth-century successors.

Henry VII's Chapel, at least, has never lacked for praise. Thomas Platter, a German in England at the end of the sixteenth century, singled out the chapel and its roof for admiration. Bacon declared that Henry VII lay buried 'in one of the stateliest and daintiest monuments of Europe, both for the chapel and for the sepulchre'. James Howell's

Londinopolis (1657) speaks of 'a chapel of admirable artificial elegancy; for a man would say that all the curious and exquisite work that can be devised is there compacted'. Evelyn's all-out attack was unusual; even Wren allowed that the chapel was 'nice embroidered work'. Evelyn and Wren's fictional contemporary, the narrator of Ned Ward's *The London Spy*, supposedly a countryman who has come up to town to see the sights, describes it rapturously as 'a chapel that may justly claim the admiration of the whole universe, such inimitable perfections are apparent in every part of the whole building, which looks so far exceeding human excellence that a man would think it was knit together by the fingers of angels, pursuant to the directions of Omnipotence'. That is a purple patch to rank beside Washington Irving's.

No doubt Henry VII's Chapel was a special case, but there is plenty of evidence that a wider affection for medieval churches lingered on. Wren's son noted that his father's design for St Paul's 'was not so well understood and relished of others, who thought it deviated too much from the old Gothic form of cathedral churches, which they had been used to see and admire in this country'. And indeed the church that Wren built was far closer to a medieval cathedral, in plan if not in style, than his first design. He gave up his idea of a centralised space; instead, St Paul's has a cruciform plan with long nave and choir, a high central vessel with side aisles, and even flying buttresses, though these are hidden behind a dummy wall and only visible from above. Throughout the classical centuries the idea lingered on in England that a Gothic gloom was the proper home of sanctity. Thus Milton in *Il Penseroso*:

But let my due feet never fail,
To walk the studious cloister's pale,
And love the high embowed roof,
With antique pillars' massy proof,
And storied windows richly dight,
Casting a dim religious light.

Milton, a Londoner, was probably inspired to this mostly by Old St Paul's and Westminster Abbey, with a bit of Cambridge thrown in.

There were other reasons for Gothic style to retain an aura of special sanctity. The Reformation was accompanied in England by two artistic phenomena: the virtual disappearance of religious or public sculpture, other than funerary sculpture; and an almost complete cessation of church-building. Tomb sculpture belonged inside churches, of course, but people noticed that it had acquired a new kind of worldliness. 'Do we affect fashion in the grave?' asks Webster's Duchess of Malfi, and Bosola replies:

Most ambitiously: princes' images on their tombs do not lie, as they were wont, seeming to pray up to heaven, but with their hands under their cheeks, as if they died of the toothache: they are not carved with their eyes fixed upon the stars, but as their minds were wholly bent upon the world, the self-same way they seem to turn their faces.

This is a complaint which would be repeated, loudly and often, in the nineteenth century, but it is interesting to find it made so early. Even at the time, where classical forms appeared in churches, they were felt to be in competition with the sacred functions of the building rather than enhancing them.

The lack of religious sculpture was a direct consequence of the Reformation: the cult of saints was now denounced as superstition; their images might or might not be tolerated, but they would certainly not be commissioned. There was probably more religious sculpture made for Henry VII's Chapel alone than for the whole kingdom in the second half of the sixteenth century. The lack of new church-building was perhaps more fortuitous. The Great Fire of 1666 led to an explosion of church-building in the City of London, mostly by Wren, and the expansion of London in the eighteenth century to more churches on the fringes, but churches built between 1550 and 1650 are a rarity. In that period Renaissance style was established as secular style, with which the great could display their wealth and magnificence. And thus, conversely, the English mind acquired and has retained the idea, alien to Italy or Central Europe, that the pointed arch is specially religious. Even in ages when the cognoscenti reckoned Gothic to be artistically inferior, people still venerated its atmosphere and associations. Howell, writing in the middle of the seventeenth century, under Cromwell's Protectorate, says that Westminster Abbey has been 'always held the greatest sanctuary and rendezvous of devotion of the whole island', a place that seems to 'strike a holy kind of reverence and sweetness of melting piety in the hearts of the beholders'. Ned Ward's London Spy, at the century's turn, 'could not behold the outside of the awful pile without reverence and amazement', viewed the interior of the 'magnificent temple' with 'equal wonder and satisfaction', and derived from the music of a service 'a taste of immortal blessings upon earth'. In the mid-eighteenth century Edmund Burke made for the Abbey and 'the moment I entered I felt a kind of awe pervade my mind, which I cannot describe; the very silence seemed sacred'. And by now another kind of awe, half sacred, half secular, was accumulating in this church, as it evolved into a pantheon of the illustrious dead.

4

DEATH'S PALACE

In the music-hall song 'The Night I appeared as Macbeth' there is a call for the author:

> 'But he's in the Abbey' –
> Then someone quite shabby
> Suggested that's where I should be.
> Shakespeare dead? Dear old Bill?
> Why, I never knew the poor fellow was ill.

Actually, Shakespeare is not at Westminster, only his statue, but so deeply is 'the Abbey' (no need to specify which) engrained in the popular consciousness as a place of interment that even someone who does not know who Shakespeare is can be supposed to know what he would be doing there. And indeed nowhere matches Westminster Abbey in the number, diversity and distinction of the famous men and women buried in it, and no place has continued to be the burial ground of the great across such a length of time. Eminent people of every century are here from the eleventh to the twentieth. They include more than two dozen English or British kings and queens, as well as the most famous Scottish monarch, Mary Queen of Scots (also Queen of France, as her tomb records) and Elizabeth Queen of Bohemia, the wife of the Winter King. No British royalty has been buried in the Abbey since George II and his immediate family, though a queen of France has (Louise, the exiled queen of Louis XVIII, later reburied in Sardinia). Louis Philippe, the last king of France, paid for the sumptuous tomb of his brother, the Duc de Montpensier. When the Prince Imperial, son of Napoleon III, was killed fighting for the British in Africa, Queen Victoria hoped for a memorial in the nave, provoking a sonnet of vitriolic opposition from Swinburne; in the event, he was commemorated in St George's, Windsor. Those inclined to romantic fantasy may toy with the notion that the Abbey also contains a rightful Emperor of Byzantium, the heir of Augustus and Constantine: that is, the Palaeologi were the last Byzantine dynasty, and a floor slab in the north transept records 'Theodorus Palaeologus 1644'. He was the eldest son of another Theodore Palaeologus, buried in a Cornish village, where his tomb sets out his descent from 'the last Christian emperor of Greece'.

English sovereigns have found their queens or consorts in many different lands. Among those lying in the Abbey are natives of what are now France, Spain, Belgium, the Netherlands, Denmark, Germany and the Czech Republic. These apart, the international presence is still striking: from France, for example, Casaubon (born in Switzerland), Saint-Évremond and Montpensier; from Germany Kneller, Handel and Salomon; from Italy Clementi. The Frenchmen were all driven into exile for political or religious reasons (why else would a Frenchman leave France?); the others liked it here. From among the Dominions Canada is represented by Bonar Law, South Africa by Joost de Blank (bishop and witness against apartheid), Australia by Gilbert Murray (classical scholar) and William McKie (master of the Abbey's music at the time of the last coronation), New Zealand by Rutherford. Though there are Americans buried in the Abbey, none is famous; Henry James and T. S. Eliot both died in London, but although each is commemorated in Poets' Corner, neither lies there.

The range of achievement laid to rest in the Abbey is unequalled. Here is a sample:

STATESMEN Elizabeth I, Chatham (Pitt the Elder), Charles James Fox, Pitt the Younger, Gladstone. (There is a cluster of Socialists in the north aisle: Sidney and Beatrice Webb, Bevin, and Attlee, the most recent prime minister buried here.)

POETS Chaucer, Spenser, Beaumont, Drayton, D'Avenant, Dryden, Prior, Campbell, Tennyson, Browning.

MEN OF LETTERS Camden, Addison, Johnson.

PLAYWRIGHTS Jonson, Congreve, Gay, Sheridan.

NOVELISTS Aphra Behn, Dickens, Hardy, Kipling.

ACTORS Ann Oldfield, Anne Bracegirdle, Garrick, Irving, Olivier. (The *Dictionary of National Biography* once noted that Garrick was the last actor to be buried in the Abbey, with the implication that it had become too exclusive for a mere player. But the whirligig of time brings in his revenges.)

GEORGE FREDERICK HANDEL Efqʳ
born February XXIII. MDCLXXXIV.
died April XIV. MDCCLIX *L.F.Roubiliac inv.et sc*

13. Roubiliac's monument to Handel, the last of his works in the Abbey, fuses heroism with frank, personal portraiture. The score held by the composer accurately transcribes the vocal line of 'I know that my redeemer liveth' from the *Messiah*.

COMPOSERS Handel and Clementi from the Continent, and besides Purcell an exceptional list of British composers: Lawes, Blow, Croft, Shield, Sterndale Bennett, Stanford, Vaughan Williams, Howells.

HISTORIANS Hakluyt, Clarendon, Macaulay, Thirlwall, Grote.

ARCHITECTS Chambers, Robert Adam, Wyatt, Scott, Pearson, Comper.

SAINTS AND HEROES OF RELIGION Edward the Confessor, Lady Margaret Beaufort, Livingstone, Dean Stanley.

FRAUDS 'Old Parr' (Thomas Parr, who died in 1635, with a claimed age of 152), James Macpherson, supposed discoverer and translator of Ossian. Both are in the south transept, among the poets and historians.

MILITARY MEN Here the picture is more mixed. From the Middle Ages there is Edward I. For the past two centuries great commanders have mostly gone to St Paul's, though Trenchard and Dowding are in the Royal Air Force Chapel at the east end. Cromwell and Admiral Blake, both interred in Henry VII's Chapel, were dug up and thrown out at the Restoration. Wolfe, the most famous soldier remembered in the Abbey and the one with the largest monument, is buried at Greenwich. One of history's famous losers, General Burgoyne, defeated at Saratoga in 1777, lies modestly in the cloisters.

SCIENTISTS A remarkable assembly, including two of the half-dozen most famous scientists ever: Newton, Hunter, John Herschel, Lyell, Darwin, J. J. Thomson, Kelvin, Rutherford.

This is a roll call only of those whose remains lie in the Abbey; if one adds those commemorated, the list is immensely extended and puts the Abbey even further ahead of any other place of commemoration. However, that is too easy: anyone can inscribe a plaque, but you can be buried only in one place. (Not quite true, of course: burial of parts of the body separately was quite common in the Middle Ages, and more recently Hardy's heart was buried in Dorset, a hundred miles from the rest of him, while Livingstone's heart remains where he died, in Africa. But the principle holds good.)

⧗

Some years ago the Engineering Council placed an advertisement in *The Times* complaining that the trouble with the country was that it failed to respect engineers enough: 'Why isn't there an Engineers' Corner in Westminster Abbey? In Britain we've always made more fuss of a ballad than a blueprint?... How many schoolchildren dream of becoming great engineers?' This provoked Wendy Cope to a memorably satiric poem, contrasting pampered poets riding around in Daimlers with engineers scraping by in cheerless garrets,

> With no hope of a statue in the Abbey,
> With no hope, even, of a modest bust.

But if the members of the Engineering Council had bothered to visit the Abbey, they would have found their profession lavishly honoured there. The reason they do not have a corner is that they have a whole aisle, a series of eminent engineers being commemorated in a line of stained-glass windows along the north of the nave (and in plaques and statues too, for that matter). The Abbey's tributes to greatness have a wide embrace.

It is true, nevertheless, that for most people Westminster Abbey is, even more than a house of kings, a place where poets lie buried. Actually, this is in part a misconception, for although a few great and several good poets do indeed lie in Poets' Corner, a majority of the many writers there commemorated have their graves elsewhere – most prominently Shakespeare and Milton. Like so much in the Abbey's history, Poets' Corner seems to have come about by accident, and then to have evolved almost organically, as though by natural process. Chaucer was buried in the east aisle in 1400, not for being a poet but presumably because he had been Clerk of the King's Works at Westminster. He was commemorated only by a lead plaque until 1568, when an admirer commissioned the present monument. Then, in 1599, Spenser was laid at the south end of the same aisle. Though he had written a famous tribute to Chaucer – 'Dan Chaucer, well of English undefiled' – his nearness to the great man may be a matter of chance; he died poor in King Street and was buried in the church close by. Again the original grave was simple and an admirer put up a monument twenty years later (the present monument is an eighteenth-century copy of this). The playwright Francis Beaumont was interred here in 1616, and his brother John, a little-known poet, eleven years later –

both below simply inscribed floor slabs. Michael Drayton joined them in 1631.

After Shakespeare's death, in 1616, William Basse wrote a commendatory poem in which he urges Spenser to nudge up closer to Chaucer and Beaumont to Spenser 'to make room/ For Shakespeare in your threefold, fourfold tomb'. But this is not quite the recognition of a poetic pantheon that it may appear, for Basse, enjoying the conceit of four literary gentlemen stuffed into one bed, adds there will hardly be a need to add a fifth between now and doomsday. He does not, therefore, imagine the south transept as a temple of fame for future masters of the English language; for him it is essentially an odd coincidence that has bundled three poets into the same corner. Ben Jonson must be responding to Basse or to someone with the same idea when he rejects the idea of putting Shakespeare in the Abbey and thus attaching his memory to a particular place:

> My Shakespeare, rise. I will not lodge thee by
> > Chaucer or Spenser, or bid Beaumont lie
> A little further to make thee a room.
> > Thou art a monument without a tomb,
> And art alive still while thy book doth live
> > And we have wits to read and praise to give.

Jonson himself was buried in the Abbey in 1637, beneath the plainest and best known of all its epitaphs – 'O rare Ben Johnson' – but in the north aisle of the nave, not in Poets' Corner. He was buried upright. According to one anecdote, he had begged the King, in his poverty, for eighteen inches of the Abbey; according to another, when the Dean of

Westminster consulted him about burial near his fellow poets, he replied that he was too poor for such a place, or for an area six foot by two. If this story is authentic, it shows that the idea of a space dedicated to poets was developing; but if so, it was not yet strong enough to secure burial there even for such a grand old man. The eighteenth century, ignoring Jonson's own sentiments, put up a wall monument to him in Poets' Corner, designed by Gibbs and executed by Rysbrack, with the celebrated epitaph repeated; but though this piece is very fine in itself, its explicitness detracts from the eloquent inexpressiveness of the actual grave (rather as Jane Austen's gravestone in Winchester Cathedral, which famously never mentions that she wrote a book, is undermined by a shiny Victorian brass plaque fulsomely spelling out her importance).

It was indeed in the earlier eighteenth century that the idea of a poets' corner firmly crystallised. Dryden, interred in 1700, was memorialised twenty years later, and Prior shortly after that. Milton got his monument in 1737, Shakespeare in 1740. These last two established the idea of a monument without a tomb – of commemoration in the south transept purely as an honour. Milton's monument also marked a victory for poetic glory over political and denominational bitterness. A friend observed to Dr Johnson, 'I have seen erected in the church a bust of that man whose name I once knew considered as a pollution of its walls.' Now a bust of the Roman Catholic Dryden stood at the north end of the aisle, of Milton at the south. What Milton himself, whose image looks suitably bleak, would have thought of it all is harder to guess. He had lived to see the Presbyterian order imposed on the Abbey by Cromwell overthrown in its turn and the

Anglican hierarchy restored; but he was also the man who had written, 'New presbyter is but old priest writ large.' His *Areopagitica* is regarded as one of the great defences of free speech and toleration, but he had explained in it, 'I mean not tolerated Popery, and open superstition.' The eighteenth century was more conciliatory, especially within the Abbey's walls.

It seems to have been around the middle of the eighteenth century, too, that this part of the church got its present nickname. A guidebook of 1766 refers to 'the Poets' Corner' as an established term. Back in 1711 Addison had spoken of 'the poetical quarter', though he had also noticed that it contained 'poets who had no monuments, and monuments which had no poets'. As with other regions whose names have no determinate origin – the Midwest, say, or the West Country – there is some vagueness about what Poets' Corner's boundaries actually are. It looks as though it originally designated only the east aisle of the south transept, though it is now commonly applied to the transept as a whole. Hawthorne enjoyed the very nookiness of the poets' quarter, on one of his visits slipping down an alley to creep into the south transept by a side door (notice how the word 'corner' is in his account even before he reaches the church):

Approaching it down Whitehall and Parliament street, you pass the Abbey, and see 'Poet's Corner' on the corner-house of a little lane, leading up in the rear of the edifice. The entrance-door is at the south-eastern end of the South Transept – not a spacious arch, but a small, lowly door – and as soon as you are within it, you see the busts of poets looking down upon you from the wall. Great poets, too...

A crucial moment in the Abbey's history as a place of burial and commemoration came with Newton's death in 1727. He was given a magnificent funeral, his body borne to the church by torchlight to lie in state in the Jerusalem Chamber; led by the Lord Chancellor, peers and ministers of the crown were among the pall-bearers. This, more than anything, encouraged the principle that the Abbey should be a resting place not only for kings and poets but for great men of every stamp. It established another idea too: that genius should be honoured publicly, and by the grandest in the land.

Foreigners were much struck by this. Voltaire, who saw Newton carried to the Abbey, wrote, 'His countrymen honoured him in his lifetime, and interred him as though he had been a king who had made his people happy.' He was moved to see monuments raised by 'the gratitude of the nation' to writers and thinkers, believing that it inspired Englishmen to greatness: 'We view their statues in that Abbey in the same manner as those of Sophocles, Plato and other immortal personages were viewed in Athens; and I am persuaded that the bare sight of those glorious monuments has fired more than one breast, and been the occasion of their becoming great men.' Learning was more honoured in England than in France, he concluded – not a claim that Frenchmen have often made. Likewise, Diderot was stirred by Poets' Corner to declare, 'In England, philosophers are honoured, respected, they rise to public offices, they are buried with the kings.' And J. W. von Archenholz, a later visitor, was astonished by the grandeur of Garrick's funeral. 'When,' he asked, 'shall we see our German actors honoured in this manner?' Voltaire had already noted that the English had buried the actress Mrs Oldfield in the Abbey with almost as much pomp as Newton; some said that they had done this merely to annoy the French, who had treated their own leading actress more scurvily, but on the contrary it showed their good sense. It was right, Voltaire concluded, to honour an art which had immortalised Sophocles and Euripides.

Ironically, the more great corpses the Abbey housed, the more people began to complain that it was not doing well enough. Oliver Goldsmith's 'Citizen of the World', an imaginary Chinese philosopher writing home with his impressions, visits 'the place of sepulture for the philosophers, heroes, and kings of England'. Spotting an especially beautiful and magnificent monument, he supposes it to be the tomb of some very great man. A king or law-giver, perhaps? No. A victorious general? No. A poet? No. So what, the Chinese asks his guide, was this man remarkable for? 'Why, sir, the gentleman that lies here is remarkable, very remarkable – for a tomb in Westminster Abbey.' Hawthorne, in turn, grumbles that there are too many nobodies buried here, so that the visitor keeps saying to himself, 'What right has this fellow among the Immortals?' But this was to misunderstand the church's history and, more subtly, to lose the complexity of its effect.

For although Westminster Abbey may be the model for the pantheons of other nations, it is not purely and simply a heroes' acre. Its force derives partly from the fact that the remains of more great achievement are here than anywhere else, but also from the way in which the dust of genius is mingled with a larger company. Voltaire notes that Newton is interred as though he were a king, Diderot that men of letters are buried with the kings; the barren dignities of a purpose-built Valhalla would not have stirred those thoughts. By a process of natural evolution that could not have been planned, the Abbey's function becomes not only honorific but integrative: it unites individual achievement to the life of society as a whole. This is well expressed by the inscription on the statue of James Watt, set up in the 1820s: after declaring him one of 'the real benefactors of the world', it continues, 'But to shew that mankind have learned to know those who best deserve their gratitude The King His Ministers and many of the Nobles and Commons of the Realm Raised this Monument...' This time, though, the King and his ministers rather overdid it. The enormous statue of Watt seated in a chair (which made Pugin, who denounced all the classical monuments, even angrier than usual) was far too large for the chapel in which it was to stand and its installation did a good deal of damage; it has since been removed to Edinburgh and the inscription copied on to a floor slab.

Even to say that men of genius are buried with kings is not enough, for they are also buried among ordinary and insignificant people. Westminster Abbey is both a pantheon and a charnel-house, and visitors have often been struck by its promiscuity. Addison entertains himself by watching a grave being dug inside the church and seeing a fragment of bone or skull thrown up with every shovelful. Defoe suggests how it was changing as a place of burial in his time, when he notes,

It is become such a piece of honour to be buried in Westminster Abbey, that the body of the church begins to be crowded with the bodies of citizens, poets, seamen and parsons, nay, even with very mean persons, if they have but any way made themselves known in the World; so that in time, the royal ashes will be thus

mingled with common dust, that it will leave no room either for
king or common people, or at least not for their monuments, some
of which also are rather pompously foolish, than solid and to the
purpose.

This comment may seem almost as tangled as the bones under the floor, treating honoured people and common people as one and the same thing, but it was more or less the truth. Ordinary people continued to be buried or commemorated in the Abbey, especially but not only in the cloisters, where we can see a tablet to 'Jane Lister, deare child' and a flagstone above the bones of an eighteenth-century plumber. As for the grander sort of 'common person' and their 'pieces of honour', the reality is that the Dean and Chapter sold spaces for monuments. An eighteenth-century Parliament voted money to build the western towers, but it was not prepared to pay for the Abbey's maintenance, and then as now a historic church had to fund itself one way or another. The idea that entombment in the Abbey should be for the great alone did not get fully established until near the end of the century.

5

······

FROM BAROQUE TO VICTORIAN

Continental sculptors dominate the Abbey's baroque period, the most prolific being Peter Scheemakers, Michael Rysbrack and Louis François Roubiliac. Native artists are present, but mostly you have to look for them. Francis Bird's monument to the German expatriate Dr Grabe and several pieces by the excellent Henry Cheere, whose work has sometimes been taken for Roubiliac's, show what English sculptors could do, but in the Abbey their comparatively modest commissions are eclipsed by the imported masters. Bird did, however, make the large monument to John Holles, Duke of Newcastle. Grinling Gibbons, born of English parents but brought up in Rotterdam, is perhaps as much Dutch as English; supreme as a decorative wood carver, he never seems quite comfortable working in stone. His monument to Sir Clowdisley Shovell offended Addison: 'Instead of the brave rough English Admiral, which was the distinguishing character of that plain gallant man, he is represented on his tomb by the figure of a beau, dressed in a long periwig, and reposing himself upon velvet cushions under a canopy of state.' The nineteenth century was to react violently against the baroque style and its conventions, but we should notice that they were under attack this early (and we have already met the protests of Webster's Bosola). There is indeed a strange dissociation at this period between sculpture in England and the rest of English visual culture. While English architecture turns away from the baroque towards a cooler Palladianism, sculpture not merely continues to be baroque but grows more so: Roubiliac's earliest monument in the Abbey, to the Duke of Argyll, who died in 1743, introduces a new degree of theatricality. In the British mind sculpture becomes an art that stands apart from the others, foreign in character and often made by foreigners too. And thus in its eighteenth-century as well as its thirteenth-century aspects, Westminster Abbey is the most continental of English buildings.

Rysbrack's masterpiece in the Abbey is the monument to Newton. Several of the larger tombs at this period were collaborations between sculptors and architects, and this one is signed by both Rysbrack and William Kent. Kent designed other monuments here, as did James Gibbs, a Scotsman trained in Rome, who could perhaps be classified as semi-baroque. These architectural tombs represent a fusion of native and continental talent. The Newton monument is grand, yet fluid, humane and even playful. 'The marble index of a mind forever/Voyaging through strange seas of thought alone' is Wordsworth's description of Roubiliac's Newton in Trinity College Chapel, Cambridge, but it would apply as well to Rysbrack's portrait, with a head that expresses both individuality and intellect. Rysbrack's lighter manner is best seen in his monument to John Gay, originally in Poets' Corner; unluckily, it was found to be blocking a medieval wall painting and has been banished to a gallery.

The Argyll monument is possibly the greatest of Roubiliac's 'allegorical machines' (as they have been called).

14. Roubiliac's monument to the Duke of Argyll brings full-blooded baroque to Westminster. Eloquence (lower left) reaches out to the spectator, while Minerva, to the right, gazes up at the Duke. Fame is writing out the Duke's titles even as we look. Incongruously, a later generation has placed to the left of the monument a medallion commemorating that arch-enemy of the baroque, John Ruskin.

No longer are the figures contained within an architectural frame. Rysbrack had made Newton recline on the top of his sarcophagus; Roubiliac's Duke dangles his leg over the edge. The figures are depicted as if in motion: Eloquence reaches forward towards the spectator, Minerva looks up at the Duke, Fame reaches out to inscribe his titles. In the most theatrical gesture of all, she is in the act of writing 'Greenwich' but has only reached the second letter; this title is left incomplete because it perished with him. The allegory has no Christian content, and Minerva at least is positively pagan. Fame has wings like an angel, though being not an angel but an abstraction she can be female, exposing a breast and a bare leg.

Roubiliac makes for the obscure General Hargrave a monument which appears to be falling down. Many of the Abbey's baroque monuments have a pyramidal shape as their background; so does this, but here the pyramid is collapsing at the Day of Judgement, while the General, naked, rises from his grave to meet his doom. Roubiliac's most famous work, his monument to Joseph and Lady Elizabeth Nightingale (1761), is equally theatrical. It borrows a device from Bernini's tomb of Alexander VII in St Peter's, Rome. This has two levels: above, the Pope kneels calmly in prayer; below, Death emerges from a door, shaking an hourglass. Roubiliac unites the two levels in a dramatic tableau. Below, the skeletal figure of Death (brilliantly carved by his assistant Nicholas Read) slithers up from his door (with real metal bolt and hinges), aiming a spear at Lady Elizabeth; Mr Nightingale darts forward in a vain attempt to protect her. The technique is dazzling – 'Here indeed the marble seems to speak and the marble seems only not alive'. Those are the

15. Roubiliac's monument to Joseph and Lady Elizabeth Nightingale.
Bernini's monument to Alexander VII in St Peter's, Rome, had shown the
pope in prayer above, and Death below. Roubiliac links the two levels of the
tomb, as Death emerges from his door and Mr Nightingale vainly tries to
ward off the spear from his wife.

words of John Wesley, who disliked most of the Abbey's tombs ('What heaps of unmeaning stone and marble!') but found in the Nightingale monument what he called 'common sense'. Wesley might be a Methodist, but he was also a man of the eighteenth century, and he could see beyond the theatricality of the work and its lack of Christian imagery to the fact that it differed from most others of its date in frankly facing the dreadfulness of death. The Victorian attitude, both High Church and Low, was to be very different.

Roubiliac's monument to Handel is perhaps the most engaging of his works, with a brio that is both grand and down to earth. The composer is shown for once not in classical costume but in modern dress, looking plump and practical, and turned in a lively posture that we can take as either sociable or heroic. 'Man is a noble animal,' says Sir Thomas Browne, 'splendid in ashes and pompous in the grave.' We can add, in duller language, that baroque conventions, at their best, balance the general and the particular. Roubiliac gives us a vivid, personal portrait of George Frederick Handel Esquire as he was in life, and ennobles him in timeless marble. This is the baroque manner at its most sophisticated.

⌛

By the end of the eighteenth century, the Abbey's status as a Valhalla was complete. 'Before this time tomorrow,' Nelson supposedly declared at the Battle of the Nile, 'I shall have gained a peerage, or Westminster Abbey.' Ironically, Nelson was to be denied the Abbey by his very greatness. The Napoleonic Wars created an enlarged demand for massive marble commemorations of military men, and only St Paul's had room for them. As Wordsworth put it, in a sonnet praising both Abbey and Cathedral, St Paul's, 'that younger Pile', was now also

> Filled with mementos, satiate with its part
> Of grateful England's overflowing Dead.

The picture of St Paul's as a repository, already glutted, for the overflow of eminent bodies may not seem very happy, but it was not far wrong. Not for the last time, Westminster Abbey had lost by its very success, and henceforth St Paul's became an outstation of Valhalla, burial place for the top brass, and even more oddly and accidentally, for painters. Reynolds had been buried there, and his successor as President of the Royal Academy, Benjamin West; Turner was given a spectacular funeral there in 1851. Leighton, Millais and Sargent followed, among others. Whereas the best-known painter in the Abbey is Kneller, who failed to climb much above the foothills of Parnassus.

Some twenty years before Nelson's glorious end at Trafalgar, Samuel Johnson's death had posed his admirers a dilemma. As he lay dying, he had asked one of his executors where he should be buried and (in Boswell's words), 'on being answered, "Doubtless, in Westminster-Abbey," seemed to feel a satisfaction, very natural to a Poet'. He was laid in the south transept, next to his friend Garrick, and a flagstone was placed over his grave, inscribed not with an eloquent epitaph such as he had written for Goldsmith's tomb, close by, but only with his name, age and date of death – but at least they are, as he would have wished, in Latin.

His friends immediately began collecting funds for a monument, but some of them began to have second thoughts: would not St Paul's be the better site? Reynolds was among those who favoured this plan, partly because he thought the space in the Abbey was too cramped, but also to encourage the Dean and Chapter of St Paul's to let sculpture into their cathedral. The vast spaces of St Paul's demanded a heroic style and manner – not to the sculptor's advantage. And so, carved by John Bacon, a marble Johnson, larger than life size and in something approximating to Roman dress, now stands as one of the four 'benefactors of the English people' who occupy the diagonals of the dome. Barefoot and bare-chested, with a scowl on his face and some indeterminate raiment wrapped around his middle, he looks all too like someone who has just leapt from the bath to answer a wrong number.

⧗

The eighteenth century transformed Westminster Abbey, the nave especially, with an odd mixture of chaos and consistency. Apart from the neoclassical junkyard under the northwest tower, the nave is pretty solidly a gallery of baroque sculpture, a mass of marble along each aisle heaving and surging almost like organic form, breaking forward from the walls, shooting up above the window sills. This sculpture gallery has often been censured as detracting from the purity of the Abbey's medieval design, and yet it could also seem, in some eyes, oddly congruous with the Gothic structure. Hippolyte Taine, visiting London in 1862, was contemptuous of most of the city's monuments, but he made an exception for the Abbey, and even felt that the tombs enhanced its atmosphere (though it is interesting that he distinguishes between the baroque sculptures and their neoclassical successors):

Superb nave, admirable Gothic architecture – the only style which suits the climate: the jumble of shapes…, the profusion of fine sculpture are required to fill this sombre atmosphere, and people the vast formlessness of dark interiors. I spent some time there, looking at monuments of the dead, a great number of graceful 18th-century sculptures, others, cold and pedantic, belonging to our own time.

A few years earlier Hawthorne had agreed that many of the monuments in the nave were ridiculous, only to change his tune:

Nevertheless, these grotesque marbles, and now obscure names, have incrusted the walls by as natural a process as that which causes the growth of moss and ivy on ancient edifices. It is the historical and biographical record of each successive age, written by itself, and all the truer for its mistakes. On the whole, I should be sorry to spare one of these monuments; and the grandeur of the Abbey is quite capable of swallowing up all these absurd individualities…

These reflections bring the historic imagination and the argument of the eye together. Half of Hawthorne wants to say that these baroque intrusions are aesthetically unfortunate, but that the price is worth paying for the sense of historical process which they convey. But he finds himself saying something rather different: that the monuments are part of the building's maturation, imparting to it the quality of organic growth, like the vegetation on those ancient walls. Horace Walpole had declared that Fingal's Cave proved 'that nature loves Gothic architecture', and the same cave reminded Theodor Fontane of Westminster Abbey. The medieval builders had broken up the aisle walls with blind arcading and stiff-leaf capitals projecting outward from the plane of the wall surface. The later monuments could almost be felt as a further outgrowth, the walls knobbly and barnacled by the accretions of time and history. And thus the organic or natural quality that people found in Gothic architecture could seem curiously consonant with the baroque. In fact, when Hawthorne visited York Minster, he thought it bare and bleak; regretting the paucity of monuments, he compared it unfavourably with the Abbey.

For our part, we can compare the Abbey with the rather different history of St Paul's, where almost all the larger monuments are neoclassical in style and early nineteenth century in date. The architecture of St Paul's and its monuments can both be grouped under the broad heading 'classical', but they are markedly unlike in aesthetic character. Wren's Roman baroque cannot quite be called either severe or florid, yet it contains a distillation of both these qualities, while the furnishings – Jean Tijou's ironwork, the woodcarving by Grinling Gibbons – are fabulously sumptuous. By contrast, the neoclassical monuments aim at a calm, marmoreal restraint. Some find them frigid, and certainly they are, if not cold, at least intentionally cool; and a kind of coolness and spaciousness is also distinctive to the version of baroque that Wren developed for his interior. But St Paul's is also very large and very grand; it demands that neoclassical sculpture lose the tame politeness that was its besetting weakness, as well as the tender charm that graces some of its smaller pieces; it enforces a monumentality of scale and composition. And thus somehow the baroque building and the neoclassical sculptures come to share or set off each other's qualities. But there is nothing organic about this: the monuments are visibly separate from the building, plonked down in front of its walls like potted palms in a conservatory.

Westminster Abbey is different. The diversity of styles is much greater and yet the baroque sculpture seems more fused with the Gothic structure, aesthetically as well as literally (the neoclassical pieces here too are another story). In some parts, undeniably, the church is overcrowded – under the north-west tower and in the aisles of the north transept, where one seems to have stumbled into a monumental mason's storeroom. There are other parts, though, where the church and its contents have perhaps achieved what Comper called 'unity by inclusion', most of all the view of the south transept's end wall, where arcade rises above arcade, culminating in the great rose window, while below there is on one side a fourteenth-century wall painting of Christ and St Thomas, on the other Roubiliac's Argyll monument – Argyll below, and the censing angels above, each equal to the best sculpture of their time, five centuries apart. It is all mysteriously harmonious. Tastes differ, but some may find in this blend of diverse aesthetic pleasures an almost improper enjoyment, like eating strawberries while listening to Bach.

Roubiliac is not quite the last of the Abbey's foreign-born sculptors, but in the next generations it will be mostly native Britons who make the monuments. As Roubiliac fades from the scene, his successors continue, for a while, in a modified baroque manner, with less bravura and pure inventiveness. Wilton's Wolfe, expiring almost nude at Quebec, and Webber's Garrick, parting the curtains for his final bow, are examples from this period. The grace of the Adam style appears in a few smaller memorials, designed by Robert Adam and executed by others. But as the eighteenth century draws to its end and the nineteenth follows, the predominant style modulates towards neoclassicism.

The last 200 years have seen a dissevering of Westminster Abbey from the best or at least the most characteristic art of the time, and the neoclassical period marks the beginning of that process. This is mildly paradoxical. It is easier to feel respect than passion for neoclassical art, but British sculpture at this period was reasonably distinguished, and the employment of native talent did not necessarily mean a retreat into parochialism. Flaxman was the first English sculptor to enjoy an international reputation, though this was principally for his drawings; and Canova himself said that Westmacott's figure of a kneeling Negro, part of the monument to Charles James Fox, was equal to any modern marble in England or France. But the neoclassical sculptors' relationship to the Abbey seems uneasy, and it is worth asking why.

Pevsner, pondering the Englishness of English art, concluded that one of its characteristics was a weakness in sculpture. The English, he thought, have a taste and talent for linear design, often of a sinuous and wayward kind, and this has unfitted them for an art which deals with the manipulation of solid mass (though he allowed Henry Moore as an exception). One might think of Blake – as it happens, one of Pevsner's examples of English sinuousness – inspired by drawing the Abbey's medieval tombs as an apprentice to the engraver Basire but putting this experience into a sculpturally influenced draughtsmanship rather than sculpture itself. Ruskin surprisingly declared that sculpture 'is essentially the production of a pleasant bossiness or round-ness of surface', and looked in it for 'beautiful surfaces limited by beautiful lines. Beautiful *surfaces*, observe.'

The nature of English sculpture was affected by the fact that for centuries so great a proportion of it was funerary and thus placed up against the walls of churches: social realities played their part, as well as genes or national character, in forming the nature of this art. But one may well feel that relief sculpture suited some of the best English neoclassicists; it brought out Flaxman's grace, sense of line and occasional charm. But in the Abbey the ambitions of patrons or the artists themselves led to an inappropriate massiveness: some of the largest monuments are too big for the building and too big for the sculptors' talents. Wilton's small bust of Admiral Temple-West is elegant and sensitive, far more pleasing than his huge Wolfe monument. Bacon's vast monument to the elder Pitt is mostly good in its individual parts but fails to compose into a satisfactory whole, and the sheer mass of blank white marble is excessive. One admires all the more the economy of Rysbrack and Roubiliac, realising that they achieve some of their grandest effects in works that are not especially large; and even a tall piece like the Argyll monu-ment has a great deal of air in it, with space and fluid move-ment between its various figures. The neoclassicists, for their part, seem to be trying to compensate for a lesser brio and panache by sheer bulk. They had to cope with three disadvantages: their style was not naturally congenial to the Gothic setting; they were working sometimes on a scale that was not congenial to themselves; and the growing lack of room for monuments was forcing them out from the walls into spaces where mountains of new marble were likely to look especially unwelcome.

Flaxman's most notable work in the Abbey, commemorating Lord Mansfield, is indeed claimed as the first monument in an English church taking the form of a free-standing group of statuary. It was executed largely by his assistants, which helps to explain why it seems noble and yet a little lifeless (Mansfield's head, carved by the master himself, has more vivacity). It is a handsome piece, but Flaxman is at his best elsewhere. Francis Chantrey, the leading sculptor of the generation after Flaxman, made several monuments for the Abbey, but again this is not where he is seen at his finest (his statue of Francis Horner is perhaps his most notable work remaining here; his huge monument to James Watt has been removed). The Abbey's sculpture was starting to lose the distinction of equalling the very best of its time.

The nineteenth century brings in the Gothic Revival, which we would expect to find conspicuous in Westminster Abbey. But here comes the surprise: there are no monuments in this style at all. Westmacott's monument to the Duc de Montpensier, who died in 1807, reverts to the medieval pattern of a figure lying upon a tomb-chest, but apart perhaps from the Duke's robe, sprinkled with fleurs-de-lys, it is entirely in the neoclassical manner, modified with touches of a domestic softness that seem to anticipate the Victorian age. Three-quarters of a century later, Dean Stanley was buried beside him, granted the rare privilege, at that date, of a free-standing tomb, and the rarer privilege of burial among the royalty of Henry VII's Chapel. Like Montpensier, he lies on a chest in the repose of death, but this piece too remains in the classical tradition.

What happened in the main church was odder. In 1852 Sir Robert Peel, that plain-spoken son of industrial Lancashire, appeared in the north transept; he was dressed in a Roman toga. By the time that Disraeli and Gladstone joined him, later in the century, that convention was hopelessly out of date, but a discomfort about modern dress persisted, and both statesmen are clad in academic or chivalric robes, conveying a vaguely classical air. These are all standing figures, placed on pedestals in front of the piers of the arcade. This arrangement was more or less forced upon the Abbey by lack of space, but it does have the effect of keeping the statues apart from the architecture. These statesmen stand in the aisle like visitors; they are not, like earlier monuments, built into the church's structure. And thus by their style and their position, and partly by accident, these pieces continue to project in a new way the old message that sculpture is the art that does not fit, the separate art. And so potent was the feeling that sculpture was essentially classical that it triumphed over the medievalism of the age, even in a medieval building.

⧗

Looking back upon the past, some of the Romantics and Victorians felt that a paradox confronted them: classical

ROBERT PEEL
BORN FEB 5 1788 DIED JULY 2 1850

16. Victorian taste found contemporary dress so out of place in sculpture that
John Gibson in 1853 wraps Sir Robert Peel in a toga, even in a medieval
church. To the left Gladstone (by Thomas Brock, 1903) hides his modernity
behind academic robes.

antiquity seemed so much closer to them than the Middle Ages. Matthew Arnold set the quaintness of Sir Walter Raleigh's *History of the World* against Thucydides, who seemed modern enough to have written yesterday. Hazlitt contrasted the archaic darkness of the Middle Ages with 'the brilliant and well-defined periods of Greece and Rome'. Oscar Wilde declared, 'Whatever, in fact, is modern in our life we owe to the Greeks. Whatever is anachronism is due to medievalism.' And in the Abbey it was literally true that the 'classical' sculpture was much more recent than the medieval.

But there was also another idea: that classical style belonged to the past and Gothic style was more consonant with the modern, romantic spirit. Winckelmann had announced that the characteristics of ancient Greek art were 'a noble simplicity and a calm greatness' – all Greek art, literature as well as sculpture. His ideas were disputed, borrowed or adapted by many others, notably by August von Schlegel, whose *Lectures on the Drama* (1807) had a great influence in Britain. Sculpture was pre-eminently the art of the ancient world, Schlegel claimed, as music is pre-eminently the art of modern times. Greek tragedy itself has a sculptural character, while modern art, of every kind, is romantic, disturbed and coloured: 'The spirit of ancient art and poetry is *plastic*, but that of the moderns *picturesque*.' And Schlegel adds an architectural analogy: 'To the application! – the Pantheon not more different from Westminster Abbey or St Stephen's in Vienna than is a play of Sophocles from one by Shakespeare.'

Westminster Abbey modern? Perhaps it was not possible to claim exactly that, but on this argument its Gothic forms are nearer to modern experience than classical forms, as Shakespeare is nearer to us than Sophocles. Henry James, present at Browning's funeral in Poets' Corner and reflecting that the occasion was one which would have rejoiced the dead man's 'irrepressible faculty for looking at human events in all sorts of slanting coloured lights', was implicitly comparing his verse, modern as it was, with the shafts of sun striking through the church's high windows. That was a flight of fancy, but in the middle of the nineteenth century Ruskin had argued that Gothic architecture was indeed the best and most functional style for modern purposes: Victorians should imitate the forms of fourteenth-century Verona not only because they were beautiful but because they were the most efficient (the pointed arch was stronger, he noted, than the horizontal lintel). In fact, he was not consistent in his argument that form should follow function: the iron and glass of railway stations and the Crystal Palace filled him with loathing. He hated the buildings of the Renaissance and even more the baroque, which he considered a symptom of moral corruption; the third volume of *The Stones of Venice*, his finest study of architecture, is an immense philippic against these styles. With magnificent inappropriateness he is commemorated in the Abbey by a bronze medallion of his head in profile placed immediately to the left of the Argyll monument, so that he stares for ever at that baroque masterpiece.

Before Ruskin there was Pugin. In the 1830s, as battle raged between the Greeks and the Goths – should modern buildings be in a classical or a medieval style? – Pugin was the Goths' fiercest and most entertaining champion. His argument had two main strands, one religious, one patriotic, and modern history has shown how potent the combination of patriotism and religion can be. First, Gothic is a Christian style, whereas classical styles are pagan. Second, Gothic is England's national style; even if classicism is tolerable in Italy, it is out of place north of the Alps. In his manifesto of 1836, *Contrasts*, Westminster Abbey has a central place. We have heard Evelyn compare St Peter's, Rome, to a list of English cathedrals and find them wanting; now Pugin reverses that judgement:

It is surprising how this edifice [St Peter's, Rome] is popularly regarded as the ne plus ultra *of a Catholic church, although as a Christian edifice it is by no means comparable to either St. Peter's of York or St. Peter's of Westminster, in both of which churches every original detail and emblem is of the purest Christian design, and* not one arrangement or feature borrowed from pagan antiquity; *and although these glorious piles have been woefully desecrated and shorn of more than half their original beauty, they yet produce stronger feelings of religious awe than their namesake at Rome, still in the zenith of its glory, with all its mosaics, gilding, and marbles.*

He contrasts the piety of medieval tombs with the paganism of later times:

The inverted torch, the club of Hercules, the owl of Minerva, and the cinerary urn, are carved, in lieu of saints and angels, on the tombs of popes, bishops, kings, ecclesiastics, statesmen, and warriors, frequently accompanied by Pagan divinities, in Pagan nudity; the pious supplication for a prayer for the soul of the deceased, is changed into a long and pompous inscription detailing his virtues and exploits.

Such monuments are less glaringly offensive in Italy, 'yet when they are intruded beneath the grand vaults of a Westminster or a Cologne, and placed by the side of the ancient memorials of the departed faithful, where every niche and ornament breathes the spirit of Catholic piety, they offer a perfect outrage to Christian feelings.' And indeed Hercules is conspicuous on Roubiliac's Warren monument, while we have already noticed Minerva admiring the Duke of Argyll. In similar spirit Christopher Wordsworth, Canon of Westminster in the middle of the nineteenth century, opposed the removal of the choir stalls to open up the transepts: the vistas would destroy all feelings of reverence by revealing worldly arrogance, fulsome epitaphs, weaponry 'breathing war and carnage in a temple of peace', a 'pantheon of pagan deities' and even nudes.

Pugin loved the Abbey, yet it might have been in as much danger from such love as from the indifference of earlier centuries. His doctrine was equivocal. On the one hand, he insists that Gothic is the right style for modern times – indeed for every time. On the other, he turns with a shudder from modernity. One of his plates in *Contrasts* shows architecture weighed in a balance: noble Gothic buildings in one scale preponderate over flimsy classical buildings in the other. The two scales are labelled fourteenth and nineteenth century. He flees from the present to the fourteenth century; and yet he believes that he can re-create the fourteenth century in his own time. He lacks a sense of history and context (in Rome he told Newman that he would like to demolish St Peter's and replace it with a new church in the Middle Pointed Style). In his eyes Westminster Abbey is like a damsel in distress, to be rescued from its persecutors. He issues a tremendous diatribe against the ways in which Dean and Chapter, Parliament and royalty have all neglected the Abbey, 'by far the finest edifice in the metropolis (if cleaned of its incongruous and detestable monuments)'. By implication, he would sweep all these memorials away. That would have meant a massive amount of resurfacing and new decoration. If Pugin had got his way, the interior might now seem almost as much Victorian as medieval. In the event, only a few particularly intrusive monuments were (sensibly enough) cut down or moved, and the rest survived.

Ruskin's attitude was quite different. In his view, buildings needed to mature, and none was at its best until a few centuries had passed over it. He detested the destructive restorations which his contemporaries inflicted on English cathedrals (where once he had described 'the great mouldering wall of rugged sculpture', he said, we should now read 'the beautiful new parapet by Mr Scott, with a gross of kings sent down from Kensington'). But he was ahead of his time. It was inevitable, anyway, that the whole of the Abbey's exterior would need renewal, because of the corrosive effects of London's sooty air. Most of the Victorian restoration, begun by Sir Gilbert Scott (he of the beautiful new parapet) and continued by J. L. Pearson, was by the standards of the time reasonably faithful and conservative, with two exceptions. The chapter house had been badly knocked about by the centuries, and Scott returned it to its medieval appearance, for the most part skilfully. Far more controversial was the reconstruction of the north transept façade, between 1875 and 1892. We have already seen how Scott replaced the porches with a more French design. That was impertinent enough, but what Pearson did above was more startling. He altered

17. The north transept, circa 1875. This photograph shows the façade as it was
before the drastic Victorian restoration (apart from the left-hand porch,
already reconstructed). The medieval design conceives the porches as
cavernous spaces hollowed out from a solid mass of wall.

18. The north transept today, after the restoration of 1875–92. Gilbert Scott has provided three gabled, projecting porches, in imitation of thirteenth-century France. Above, J. L. Pearson has removed the rose window, itself an early eighteenth-century replacement by William Dickinson, and substituted an inferior design of his own.

the blind arcading in the gable, for no apparent reason. Most shockingly, he replaced the existing rose window (early eighteenth century, by Dickinson, but fairly close to the original) with a much inferior design. (The eighteenth-century stained glass was kept, though it no longer fitted, and the Apostles had to have their feet chopped off.)

Pearson was a very fine architect and it is a pity (and puzzling) that he chose to blot his escutcheon in this way. But this episode marks a change of taste, because it was so fiercely criticised, above all by William Morris, who had founded the Society for the Protection of Ancient Buildings to fight the harshness and insensitivity of High Victorian restoration. Ruskin's spirit was beginning to prevail. Morris, who did not believe in understatement, declared that the Abbey was 'our most beautiful building' and second to none among the marvels of the Middle Ages. Yet of the exterior he said, 'A long series of blunders of various kinds, all based on a false estimate of the true value of the building, have damaged it so vitally, that scarcely any of its original surface remains, and we have nothing left us but a mere outline, a ghost, so to say, of what it was.' W. R. Lethaby, Pearson's successor as surveyor and another remarkable architect in his own right, was to echo this when he wrote, 'The exterior has been so completely recased that to describe it will be to describe a series of modern works. Save for the mass, and a certain grace of general form, only the interior can concern us as an authentic work of ancient Art.' Morris had disliked the eighteenth-century restoration of the north transept, but at least it had possessed character, he said, and was pleasingly weathered. The monuments inside, however, were 'disastrous and disgraceful', 'the most hideous specimens of false art that can be found in the whole world', 'they make us a laughing-stock among the nations'. But even so he did not think that they should be removed: they were so integrated into the building that a 'thorough restoration' would be still worse. History could not be unmade.

6

THE ABBEY IMAGINED

Although Westminster Abbey is more unified in style than almost all English cathedrals, it has always seemed to be divided into different regions. In the Middle Ages a screen, called a pulpitum, divided the western part of the nave from the area of monastic worship. After the Reformation, the eastern parts acquired a new distinctiveness: you had to pay to get into them. Before 1600 Donne was already writing about 'the man that keeps the Abbey tombs', who for a fee would guide you round the kings of England. This sounds like private enterprise; in due course, the Dean and Chapter were to charge visitors more systematically. A nineteenth-century Dean and Chapter cut the price, in order to seem more welcoming, but the division between free and enclosed areas remained, diminished only in the late twentieth century, since when, in effect, you have had to pay to get into the church at all.

Such mundane practicalities have their effects on how a building is experienced – effects that in this case were enhanced by the way that the nave was reordered in the eighteenth century. Newton's monument was placed against the left side of the screen dividing the nave from the choir; Stanhope's monument matches it symmetrically on the other side. John Conduitt, who was married to Newton's niece, not only organised his uncle's memorial but arranged for his own monument at the west end of the nave, facing Newton. This too is balanced symmetrically, on the other side of the door, by another memorial. All four monuments are similarly composed, with figures against a pyramidal backdrop; Rysbrack made the eastern pair and Cheere the western. The screen itself was a modern work, designed by Nicholas Hawksmoor, and plain in style, so that Newton and Stanhope stood out strongly against it, dominating the nave. This effect more or less disappeared in the 1830s, when Blore's screen (gaudily regilded in the twentieth century) replaced Hawksmoor's, half hiding the tops of the pyramids behind Gothic elaboration; the modern gilding makes the screen dominate the sculptures even more. But in the middle of the eighteenth century the pattern of these monuments, answering each other across the length of the nave, had the effect of articulating the nave as a separate area, and one with a distinctive function (see endpapers). Francis Atterbury, the Jacobite dean who had been stripped of his office and condemned to exile, was buried by the west door, having asked to lie 'as far from Kings and Kaesars as the space will admit of'. There was now a royal abbey, hidden from immediate view, accessible only on payment of a fee, site of ancient tombs and chivalry; and there was a public abbey, the place of modern commemoration.

Many eighteenth- and nineteenth-century accounts of the Abbey perceive it as having three or four distinct regions: the nave, the sanctuary, the eastern area and Henry VII's Chapel. Pugin appreciates the effect of the wonders of Henry VII's Chapel breaking newly upon the eye after the visitor's survey might seem to have been complete, 'at the *extreme end* of a church of immense length'. Until well into the nineteenth century, the closing off of the eastern parts gave them an air of especial desolation. For Washington Irving in 1819 a visit to the Abbey as a whole is a journey into the past, but the eastern area plunges him into a still-deeper antiquity, drawing him into a reverie of fable and romance and paladins whose exploits are 'between the history and the fairy tale'. Thirty-five years on, things have changed: Hawthorne, having paid sixpence for a guided tour, finds himself hustled around too quickly to take anything in properly – a surprisingly modern experience. As early as the 1830s, even before the railways could have had much effect, Pugin inveighs against the vulgar trippers 'who come to inspect this church, and the feelings with which they perambulate its sacred aisles – a mere flock of holiday people who come to London to see sights, and take the Abbey on their way to the Surrey Zoological Gardens'. It is difficult to tell how much the Abbey was frequented in the eighteenth century. Engravings of the nave show a bare expanse with only a couple of visitors or a few strollers chatting together, but the artists may merely have wanted to give the scale without cluttering up the picture. If we were to judge from the photographs in modern books, we would conclude that the Abbey had no visitors at all. But the solitary contemplation of mortality, a prominent theme in earlier accounts of the place, does fade from them by the middle of the nineteenth century.

Countless visitors have described Westminster Abbey, but all too often, it must be admitted, their sentiments are stale and conventional. With more talented writers it can be hard to tell authenticity from artifice. In an essay on honour, Addison picks out a phrase from the epitaph on the Newcastle monument in the north transept: 'a noble Familie for all the Brothers were Valiant and all the sisters Virtuous'. A century later, Washington Irving finds the Gothic tombs vastly superior to the fanciful and overwrought 'modern monuments' – in appearance, and in their inscriptions also. The medievals, he says, had a noble way of 'saying things simply, and yet saying them proudly; and I do not know an epitaph that breathes a loftier consciousness of family worth and honourable lineage, than one which affirms, of a noble house, that "all the brothers were brave, and all the sisters virtuous"'. Irving has in fact misquoted, losing the alliterative echo in 'valiant... virtuous', which makes a link between masculine and feminine excellences in the very act of distinguishing them. And he cites the epitaph as an example of the proud simplicity of the Middle Ages, although it actually comes from one of the baroque monuments that he deplores. His sentiments, at this moment, seem to be borrowed from books rather than found for himself. Hawthorne too, entering the Abbey for the first time, notes an 'antique tomb' and its words about valiant brothers and virtuous sisters; and though he is writing in his private notebooks, one suspects that his discovery is not as spontaneous as he lets it appear. A visitor today may be equally struck by the words with which the inscription continues: 'This Dutches was a wise, wittie and learned Lady, which her many Bookes do well testifie' – an early and ungrudging tribute to a woman's intellect. This duchess also once wrote that she was very ambitious, not for beauty, wealth or power but to be raised 'to Fame's tower, which is to live by remembrance in after-ages'. Well, she is remembered here.

Clichés have their uses: received opinions tell us what people commonly felt, or at least expected to feel. Many descriptions of the Abbey, across the centuries, evoke the melancholy of the place, and the idea that perhaps returns more persistently than any other is gloom. In the course of the nineteenth century, though the notes of desolation and decay pass away from these accounts, the sense of sombre darkness if anything seems to thicken. Both these changes correspond to a reality: the Abbey was recovering a more vigorous liturgical life and the soot was multiplying in the London air. Several nineteenth-century writers declare that the church's interior is built of brown stone (even 'rich brown stone'), but the colour that they were admiring was mostly not stone but grime. Gilbert Scott, in an ill-judged attempt at conservation, coated much of the interior with shellac. This not only sealed in the existing dirt, but attracted more.

For Addison the Abbey is entirely a memento mori, a site for meditation upon death and transience:

> *When I am in a serious humour, I very often walk by myself in Westminster Abbey; where the gloominess of the place, and the use to which it is applied, with the solemnity of the building, and the condition of the people who lie in it, are apt to fill the mind with a kind of melancholy, or rather thoughtfulness, that is not disagreeable.*

It is interesting that he sees only one use for the building, and that is to house the dead; he has no sense that it might do anything for the living, apart from inspiring them to an imaginative fellowship with those who live no more. At the beginning of the twentieth century Ford Madox Ford's voice is much more vehement, turning gloom to grimness and brown to black:

> *In the black and dismal cloisters of our Valhalla… there, where the great towers rise up, grim and black, where the memorials cower at the base of walls grim and black, where fountains stand in the weeping light of obscure and useless cloisters that suggest the gaunt and blackened skeletons of obsolete faiths, obsolete pursuits, obsolete hopes and obsolete despairs; where there are all sorts of courts and alleys of old houses that seem to whisper of faded virtues, faded vices, faded pleasures, dead crimes…* [and so on for some time]

This is pretty coarse stuff, but it must have borne some resemblance to the physical reality, and its rather tired rhetoric does echo what earlier visitors had less crudely said. For John Wesley, as for Addison, a visit was an exercise in sobriety: 'I once more took a serious walk through the tombs in Westminster Abbey,' he told his diary in February 1764. Karl Philipp Moritz, a German visitor to England in 1782, wrote, 'I saw Westminster Abbey on a dark and melancholy day, in keeping with the character of the place.' Dickens's Uncommercial Traveller, wandering through the city on a damp, cold night in March, comes to the Abbey and finds it 'fine gloomy society… suggesting a wonderful procession of its dead among the dark arches and pillars'. Washington Irving chooses the fall of the year for his pilgrimage, 'one of those sober and rather melancholy days, in the latter part of

Autumn, when the shadows of morning and evening almost mingle together, and throw a gloom over the decline of the year... There was something congenial to the season in the mournful magnificence of the old pile.' The words that echo through his essay are 'mournful', 'solemn', 'sad', 'mysterious', 'awful', 'deserted', 'quiet', 'noiseless'; but recurrent are 'melancholy', and 'gloom' and 'gloomy' most of all.

By the time that Hawthorne reached the Abbey, it had mostly lost the air of loneliness and neglect; in fact he noted on his first visit, rather surprisingly, that it appeared to be in perfect repair. But he too remarks and takes pleasure in the church's gloom, even on a bright day: admiring the soaring pillars, he says, 'It was beautiful to see the sunshine falling in among them, and lightening up their aged gloom with the cheerfulness of the summer afternoon.' It is as though the sombreness were intrinsic to the building, and the shafts of light a passing and partial tempering of an almost palpable obscurity. And indeed when he saw St Paul's, he contrasted its lucidity with the nature of a Gothic church, 'so dim and mysterious, with its narrow aisles, its intricacy of pointed arches, its dark walls, and columns and pavement, and its painted glass-windows, bedimming even what daylight might otherwise get into its eternal evening'. He was not yet aware how much his idea of Gothic depended on one building and its setting – Westminster Abbey, darkened by centuries of London smoke. Later, when he had seen the cathedrals at York and Worcester, he would come to realise the variety of Gothic effect. He would also enjoy a more deeply crepuscular Abbey on a foggy November day when it was almost invisible from outside; he describes entering 'those holy precincts, which looked very dusky and grim in the smoky light', and looking 'upward at the fog which hung half-way between us and the lofty roof of the Minster'. It is a scene that may remind one of mountains in a Chinese painting – a great height rising through a wreath of cloud.

Goldsmith's imaginary Chinese visitor, for his part, speaks of the 'gloom' that the 'venerable remains of deceased merit' inspire. He calls the Abbey 'a temple marked with the hand of antiquity, solemn as religious awe, adorned with all the magnificence of barbarous profusion, dim windows, fretted pillars, long colonnades, and dark ceilings'. Henry James, too, delighted in the 'dim transepts' and 'rich dusk'. But this older experience of the Abbey has entirely passed away. Cleaning has made the stone pale again. Even the climate has changed: Clean Air Acts and central heating have abolished the London fogs of yesteryear, and the Gothic evening has proved not to be eternal after all. But in the later Victorian age the feeling persisted that twilight and winter were the Abbey's proper season. A moment during Stanley's deanship brings out the commingling of the church's ancient darkness with its more recent vitality. It was the last day of 1876, a few hours before the Queen would be proclaimed in India under her new title of Empress. The Dean and the Prime Minister, Disraeli, slipped privately into the north transept, which was 'crowded to excess' (it was a Sunday and Frederick Farrar was preaching). 'I would not have missed the sight for anything,' Dizzy declared, 'the darkness, the lights, the marvellous windows, the vast crowd, the courtesy, the respect, the devotion – and fifty years ago there would not have been fifty persons there.' The Orient was in his mind, he told Stanley, who responded by comparing their presence in the crowd to the tales of Haroun al Raschid moving incognito through

Baghdad by night. 'I like these Haroun al Raschid expeditions,' said the Prime Minister. In this little episode the Abbey is seen, yet again, not only as a spiritual oasis in the secular city, but also as importing the poetry of the exotic into London's prose.

Across the generations the Abbey's visitors have felt its sounds and its daily business as part of its being. To stand or sit or move in a great living church is not totally a visual experience; it is also an experience of volume, sensed as well as seen (as blind men can sense the disposition of objects in a room), and at best an experience for the ears also. I have quoted Milton's evocation of studious cloisters, tall pillars and Gothic vaulting in *Il Penseroso*. This is how he continues:

> There let the pealing organ blow,
> To the full voic'd choir below,
> In service high, and anthems clear,
> As may with sweetness, through mine ear,
> Dissolve me into ecstasies,
> And bring all heav'n before mine eyes.

The man who wrote in *Areopagitica* that he could not praise a fugitive and cloistered virtue does not, in this poem, retreat into a holy silence. Sound – more than sound, loud noise – infuses the Gothic evocation of heaven upon earth.

For Ned Ward, similarly, it is music in the Abbey which offers a foretaste of heaven. As his narrator, the countryman come up to town, strolls in the nave, admiring the architecture and antiquities, he describes himself as entertained, satisfied, engaged, astonished; but when the bell begins to chime for afternoon prayers and the choir is opened, his tone changes:

There our souls were elevated by the divine harmony of the music, far above the common pitch of our devotions, whose heavenly accents have such an influence upon the contrite heart that it strengthens our zeal, fortifies the loose imagination against wandering thoughts, and gives a man a taste of immortal blessings upon earth, before he is thoroughly prepared for the true relish of celestial comforts.

(A cosy form of contrition, though, we may think, especially as he continues, 'When we had given our souls the refreshment of this enlivening exercise…')

Macaulay called the Abbey a 'temple of silence'. To Burke in the Abbey 'the very silence seemed sacred' – but silence in a large building, above all a large building in a city, can seem almost palpable: it is enjoyed as the felt absence of sound. Washington Irving extracts an agreeable melancholy from the Abbey's silence: 'Nothing impresses the mind with a deeper feeling of loneliness, than to tread the silent and deserted scene of former throng and pageant.' But he does not actually mean that he hears nothing: rather, he feels the Abbey to be a container of silence, holding its silence within itself, while the sounds that reach his ear belong elsewhere, for he contrasts the 'gloomy vaults and silent aisles' with the occasional rumours of the secular world penetrating this religious space, 'the sound of busy existence, … the rumbling of the passing equipage; the murmur of the multitude; or perhaps the light laugh of pleasure'. The church's walls seem as rigid, and as paper-thin, as the boundary between life and death. We realise how profoundly different a visit to the Abbey was then from the tourist jostle of today as Irving describes the 'strange effect upon the feelings, thus to hear the surges of active life hurrying along and beating against the very walls of the sepulchre'.

But Irving also appreciates that the Abbey's own sounds are part of its being. Even the reverberation of the clock, heard from the cloisters, is not mere abstract sound but a speaking voice, with a tale to tell, 'a warning of departed time sounding among the tombs'. Within the church itself, he takes pleasure in 'the distant voice of the priest repeating the evening service, and the faint responses of the choir', and discourses at some length on the rolling and billowing sonority of the organ, the singers' soaring voices – rather conventional, second-hand raptures, to be frank. What is more interesting is that he feels this music not as counteracting the Abbey's ancient gloom but as in harmony with it, enhancing it. On this winter evening, the service is a space of sound and slight illumination within the cavernous darkness of the building as a whole, lit by tapers, with the choristers as small patches of white against the deep brown of their oaken stalls.

In the High Victorian age Hawthorne finds the Abbey engaged with the buzz and hum of London life, not separated from it. This was partly perhaps because the Abbey's ministry had grown more vigorous in the meantime, and partly because the building is multiply suggestive, so that the pilgrim can pick his own moral. At the time of his first visit, London happened to be celebrating victory at Sebastopol: he could hear the boom of cannon penetrating the church's interior, and reflected wryly that this latest success was likely to add more 'laurelled tombstones' to those he had already seen. On a later occasion, he heard again the Abbey bells 'clamorous for joy, chiming merrily, musically, obstreperously – the most rejoicing sound that can be conceived; and we ought to have a chime of bells in every American town and village, were it only to keep alive the celebration of the Fourth of July'. He supposed that this must be to mark another victory over the Russians, only to find that these were wedding bells: 'The last time I was there, Westminster was flinging out its great voice of joy for a national triumph; now, for the happy union of two lovers. What a mighty sympathyzer is the old Abbey!'

This notion of the church as a 'mighty sympathiser', of it speaking with a 'voice' – of joy or of grief – is echoed by many of those who have written about it. The idea recurs that the Abbey not only inspires emotions but feels and enacts them itself, as though it were a living being. One of the congregation at the coronation of George VI recorded, 'I thought it all *very, very* wonderful and I expect the Abbey did, too. The arches and beams at the top were covered with a sort of haze of wonder..., at least I thought so.' The writer was the eleven-year-old Princess Elizabeth, and the next coronation would be her own ('At the end the service got rather boring,' she added, 'as it was all prayers.'). In 1941, when a bomb crashed through the crossing, scattering debris, the Dean, who lost all his own possessions to enemy action, declared, 'When all is said and done, the Abbey, which is England, must suffer with England.' Like St Paul's rising above the fires of the Blitz, or the damaged wing of Buckingham Palace and the Queen's assertion that now she could look the East

End in the face, the photographs of the wounded Abbey were offered as part of the national passion.

Most people today, at a guess, think of the Abbey as primarily a place of memory and public ritual, but in the past, when it was emptier and dingier, it was seen pre-eminently as a place of death. The long poem with which John Dart prefaced his *Westmonasterium* (1723), the first large scholarly study of the Abbey, dwells upon sober and funerary thoughts ('Away, sportive Venus'). He has no patriotic or heroic emphasis; instead, he lingers over dusty tombs, gilded with coloured light from the stained-glass windows, and jackdaws nesting among the battlements. He is also struck that the kings are buried where they are crowned; in their hour of glory let them remember the 'second visit' to come. This had long been a commonplace: Jeremy Taylor, for example, in his *Holy Dying*, had observed that 'where our kings have been crowned, their ancestors lay interred, and they must walk over their grandsire's grave to take his crown. There is an acre sown with royal seed, the copy of the greatest change, from rich to naked, from ceiled roofs to arched coffins, from "living like gods" to "die like men".' And Waller wrote of the Abbey:

> It gives them crowns, and does their ashes keep;
> There made like gods, like mortals there they sleep;
> Making the circle of their reign complete,
> Those suns of empire, where they rise, they set.

One of the earliest poems on the Abbey is a sonnet by Thomas Bastard, published in 1598:

When I behold, with deep astonishment,
To famous Westminster how there resort,
Living in brass or stony monument,
The princes and the worthies of all sort:
Do not I see reformed nobility,
Without contempt, or pride, or ostentation,
And look upon offenceless majesty,
Naked of pomp or earthly domination?
And how a play-game of a painted stone,
Contents the quiet now and silent sprites,
Whom all the world which late they stood upon,
Could not content nor quench their appetites.
　　Life is a frost of cold felicity
　　And death the thaw of all our vanity.

In part this is just – the tombs of the earlier kings and queens do indeed seem purified of pride and contempt; but it also suggests that sententiousness can overcome the plain evidence of the senses. Some of these worthies are surely 'pompous in the grave', and the most recent tombs had certainly not renounced pride and ostentation. A poem probably by Francis Beaumont, perhaps the most famous written about the Abbey, was composed a little later:

Mortality, behold and fear,
What a change of flesh is here!
Think how many royal bones
Sleep within this heap of stones,

> Hence removed from beds of ease,
> Dainty fare, and what might please,
> Fretted roofs, and costly shows,
> To a roof that flats the nose:…

Even this is a half-truth, for these royal bones could also be said to sleep beneath fretted roofs more splendid than had covered them in life. Bacon noted that Henry VII 'dwelleth more richly dead, in the monument of his tomb, than he did alive in Richmond or any of his palaces'.

Washington Irving, two centuries on, is more florid:

What, thought I, is this vast assemblage of sepulchres but a treasury of humiliation; a huge pile of reiterated homilies on the emptiness of renown, and the certainty of oblivion! It is indeed the empire of death; his great shadowy palace; where he sits in state, mocking at the reliques of human glory, and spreading dust and forgetfulness on the monuments of princes.

And anticipating Macaulay's famous picture of the New Zealander leaning on a broken arch of London Bridge to sketch the ruins of St Paul's, he looks forward to a time when wind will whistle through the Abbey's broken arches, owls hoot from the shattered tower and ivy twine round the fallen columns. Well, it is true that nothing lasts for ever: the Pyramids have endured for four and a half thousand years, and may for thousands more, but even they will perish one day, and so will Westminster Abbey. Yet we might now be more inclined to think that the Abbey resists oblivion; and Irving's moralising meditation is more time-bound than he knows. It is inspired by the dust and decay of the building in his own time, and his unconscious assumption that this is a continuous process. Today, when the Abbey is cleaned, restored and regilded, we are more likely to think in terms of recovery.

In any case, the idea that the Abbey was a sermon upon the vanity of earthly glory always had to compete with another: that it softened the asperity of death. We have heard Addison say that it encouraged a thoughtfulness that was not disagreeable. Jeremy Taylor gave a consoling twist to the mortality of monarchs: 'When we die, our ashes shall be equal to kings, and our accounts easier, and our pains... shall be less.' For Irving to enter the Abbey was to travel in time, to be carried into a remote antiquity, but in other minds the place abolished time. Reading the dates on the tombs of some who had died yesterday and some 600 years before, Addison thought of the Day of Judgement, 'when we shall all of us be contemporaries, and make our appearance together'.

Like Addison, Irving was impressed by the sheer jumbled multitude of the Abbey's dead; one almost smiles, he says, 'to see how they are crowded together and justled in the dust'. A visit inspired in Dickens the grotesque thought that if all the dead were raised in the night, there would be no room in the streets for the living to come out into. And indeed the numbers buried here are very large – 4,000 by one estimate, many more by another – so that in the twentieth century the decision was made that only ashes could now be accepted for burial. But the 'curiosity shop' element of the Abbey, the busy jostling for place, has the odd effect of making these dead seem closer to life. The contrast is great with the marmoreal chilliness of other pantheons. Poets' Corner adds to the effect in its own way. Irving noted that visitors lingered there longest, though the monuments were mostly simpler than elsewhere: it is as though one were among 'friends and companions; for indeed there is something of companionship between the author and the reader'. So even he imagines the boundaries between past and present dissolved and a fellowship uniting the dead with the living. Dickens imagined a wonderful procession of the Abbey's dead, 'each century more amazed by the centuries following it than by all the centuries going before'. The place struck Henry James, attending Browning's funeral in Poets' Corner, 'not only as local but social – a sort of corporate company; so thick… is the population of its historic names and figures'. Imagining the dead scrutinising the claims of each new arrival, he fancied that Browning himself would have enjoyed the questioning among the other poets, and even the slight buzz of scandal to which his interment might give rise. He thought back also to Macaulay's description: 'that temple of silence and reconciliation where the enmities of twenty generations lie buried'. Hawthorne had found in Poets' Corner an interest in the presence of dead people – and 'presence' is a telling choice of word – which he had never found anywhere else. Like James, he delighted in the fancy of a social experience, 'the consciousness (mingled with a pleasant awe) of kind and friendly presences, who are anything but strangers to you, though heretofore you have never personally encountered them'; like Addison, he thought of them all as contemporaries, and like Macaulay, he imagined old wounds being healed: 'One is pleased, too, at finding them all there together, however separated by distant generations, or by personal hostility or other circumstances, while they lived.'

And indeed, some of the Abbey's juxtapositions are

piquant, some moving. We have already seen Elizabeth buried in the same tomb as her sister, Mary, and opposite Mary Queen of Scots. The statues of Gladstone and Disraeli stand by adjacent columns, like boxers before the bell, half turned towards each other but not catching the other's eye. Macaulay is across the aisle from Dryden, whom he condemned for apostasy. Thirlwall and Grote, the two historians of Greece, the one a liberal bishop, the other a philosophic radical, banker and MP, lie next to each other. Macpherson, who faked the poems of Ossian, rests very close to Johnson, who denounced the imposture. And Johnson lies as near to Garrick as when they had set out together from Staffordshire for London to make their way in the world, with one horse between them.

7

THE CHURCH IN THE CITY

Looking at Westminster Abbey from outside, we might wish to say that it expresses a meaning unchanged for 700 years: it was built for the worship of God, and that remains its daily business. But there is another sense in which its external meaning has altered, not because the building itself has altered (though it has), but because London has altered around it.

The earliest depiction of the Abbey, on the Bayeux Tapestry, shows a man, holding a weathercock, crossing from the Palace of Westminster to the Abbey at roof level on a sort of gangway. Whatever else this figure is meant to signify, he also declares the intimate connection between royal and religious Westminster: church and palace are read as two elements of a single complex. Medieval Westminster was an enclave, enclosed and surrounded by water, with the Thames to the east and the River Tyburn formed into a moat around the other sides. We can get some sense of what it was like from one or two cathedral closes. At Salisbury, for example, one must enter the close from the town through an arched gate, and one suddenly finds oneself, with almost the inconsequence of a dream, in a new and spacious place, with the suggestion of water close at hand. Wells is the most complete

19. The eleventh-century Abbey depicted on the Bayeux Tapestry. On the right, Edward the Confessor is borne to his funeral. To the left, a figure plants a weathercock on the church, his pose demonstrating the intimate connection between the Abbey and Palace of Westminster.

survival in Europe of a non-monastic cathedral with its associated buildings – church and moated palace (the nearness of water yet again) and the houses of the singing men. Westminster must have had something of this flavour. As at Norwich or Salisbury still, there will have been the paradox of an inner city more broad and open than the outer town around it.

The medieval town or village of Westminster clustered round the royal and monastic enclave, a noisome slum of narrow alleyways. But the sixteenth century saw the beginnings of a change, even before the monastery was dissolved. Several times the Abbey's significance in the life of London and even of the nation has been affected by fire – not in the church itself, but beyond. In 1512 fire gutted the Privy Palace, which formed the southernmost part of the rambling sequence of buildings that made up the Palace of Westminster. This put an end to the palace as a royal residence, and Henry VIII developed Whitehall instead as his London base. In 1547 Henry suppressed religious colleges, including the College of St Stephen, which was part of the palace complex, and thus another interpenetration of the royal and the religious at Westminster came to an end. St Stephen's Chapel became the regular meeting place for the House of Commons, while the Lords used part of the old Privy Palace. Westminster Hall continued as a law court, and a further court was built beside it under Elizabeth. By the end of the century a disposition was established which in one way or another has continued ever since: law and legislation to the east of Old and New Palace Yards, royalty and religion to the west.

In 1600 a young visitor from Bohemia, Baron Waldstein, recorded in his diary:

20. Westminster in the mid-sixteenth century, in a nineteenth-century copy
taken from Anthonis van den Wyngaerde's panorama of London. Though
linked to London, Westminster still has a separate character, with open
country beyond. The Abbey appears as a riverside church, towering over the
buildings around it.

Went along the Thames to the small town of Westminster.
Although it is over a mile from the City, we went past buildings
the whole way. The place gets its name from being situated on the
western side of the City, and it is famous for its Abbey, its Court
of Justice, and its Palace. The Abbey, one of the finest in the whole
of England, is most magnificent and also very beautiful; it is
renowned as the place of the coronation of the Kings of England
and as their place of burial. It contains a large number of chapels
and some very splendid royal monuments.

Although Westminster is now part of the capital city's urban area, it still feels like its own place, and like a riverside place. And Waldstein sees it as a royal, religious and administrative cluster, the Abbey itself being described in purely royal, not national terms.

For Drayton too, in his poetical survey of England, *Poly-Olbion* (1613–22), Westminster is a riverside complex, seen from the Thames. And it is two things, church and palace:

> Then Westminster the next great Thames doth entertain,
> That vaunts her palace large and her most sumptuous fane:
> The land's tribunal seat that challengeth for hers,
> The crowning of our kings, their famous sepulchres.

In this account the royalty has been sucked out of the palace (it is described as a law court), while the Abbey, again, is purely royal. In Donne's satire, written in the 1590s, the Abbey is still a place of kings, and of kings exclusively, even though other wealthy citizens had in fact begun to intrude their monuments by now:

He, like to a high stretched lute string squeaked, 'O Sir,
'Tis sweet to talk of kings.' 'At Westminster,'
Said I, 'the man that keeps the Abbey tombs,
And for his price doth with whoever comes,
Of all our Harrys, and our Edwards talk,
From king to king and all their kin can walk:
Your eyes shall hear naught, but kings; your eyes meet
Kings only; the way to it, is King Street.'

Imagination and politics, as well as physical form, affect the
way in which the urban fabric is read. Edmund Waller,
looking back after the Civil War, sees the Abbey and the
Palace of Westminster not as parts of one royal and religious
complex but as opponents facing one another:

When others fell, this, standing, did presage
The crown should triumph over popular rage;
Hard by that house where all our ills were shaped,
The auspicious temple stood, and yet escaped.

In 1698 fire again affected the Abbey's history, when most
of Whitehall Palace burnt down. The result was to evacuate
royalty from the area altogether, as the King removed himself
to St James's and Hampton Court. Whitehall itself developed
as an elegant suburb at London's west end, lined with large
modern residences; the Abbey was now on the edge of a fashionable district. Its crumbling fabric and unfinished west front
were a reproach to the area, and in 1732 Parliament voted the
money for the towers to be completed. The architect was
Nicholas Hawksmoor, pupil of Wren, who had himself made
designs for central and western towers many years before.

This was a place where Hawksmoor's eccentric originality could easily have been out of place, but the executed design (finished after his death) is well behaved. He made his towers slightly narrower than their lower parts, giving them lightness and grace. They are Gothic (Beverley Minster was the main model) but they do not pretend to be medieval; engagingly, Hawksmoor mixes in classical or baroque details – the volutes supporting the pinnacles, the cornices between the areas of panelling and, most obviously, a pair of broken pediments at the level of the gable. The final result is very pleasing, dignified without pomposity. The west front is both serious and (in some of its details) witty. It is not sublime or romantic, nor does it possess the fusion of logic and tenderness expressed in the west front of Notre-Dame in Paris, but otherwise it has almost all that one could want in a façade. It is ironic, though, that this façade is what everyone first thinks of when they think of Westminster Abbey, as it is quite unlike the building as a whole.

⌛

Part of the thrill of the Piazza Navona in Rome is the way that you must approach it through narrow lanes, before suddenly breaking through into its vast, radiant space. The piazza of St Peter's was once like that, with Bernini's curving colonnades seeming to thrust back the thick tangle of an older Rome, before Mussolini tore down the medieval lanes to make the present boring boulevard. And in a more modest way, the approach to Westminster Abbey must have shared some of this quality. Ned Ward's London Spy comes to it from the delectable spaciousness of St James's Park, passing through a 'narrow passage' and emerging into the Broad Sanctuary. This open space to the north of the church was a fraction of the size of the present Parliament Square, so that one suddenly came upon the Abbey towering abruptly above, 'raised to such a stupendous height'. In the eighteenth century the Abbey had become part of a dense urban fabric. Houses pressed against its northern flank and around the parish church of St Margaret, situated just north of its eastern limb. To the east, Henry VII's Chapel thrust its nose out through a line of handsome modern residences. Old Palace Yard was a rectangle tightly enclosed between the Abbey and the palace; New Palace Yard was a similar area between Westminster Hall and the residential district to the north.

Most visitors are likely to have come to the Abbey from Whitehall, to the north. At this time Whitehall stretched from where Trafalgar Square is now as far as the present Downing Street, where buildings blocked its further progress. Unusually wide for London, it must have seemed halfway between a street and an elongated piazza, rather like the Broad in Oxford today. From the end of Whitehall one continued along the older, much narrower King Street (as in Donne's day: 'The way to it, is King Street'), which led directly to the end of the north transept, looming ever larger above one. It was a dramatic approach.

Another route from the centre of town was by river. Standing on Westminster Bridge in 1802, Wordsworth could declare that that 'Earth has not anything to show more fair', a judgement which now seems incomprehensible. But in the mid-eighteenth century London was perhaps, after Venice, as beautiful as any city in Europe. Looking away from Westminster, Canaletto painted the great curve of the river

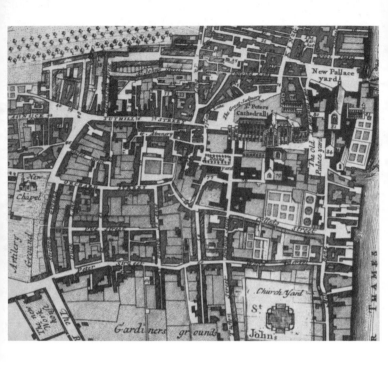

21. In this early eighteenth-century map Westminster Abbey is surrounded by a tight urban fabric. Beyond Broad Sanctuary, to its north, is a dense network of alleys and houses, since cleared to form Parliament Square. To its east, Old Palace Yard still has the character of an enclosure inside the complex of palace and abbey.

with the city gathered above it, crowned by the majestic bulk of St Paul's. Turning the other way, he painted the line of river up to the Abbey, with the twin towers forming a new focal point, and fields and woodland beyond. Westminster Bridge, London's second crossing of the Thames, was built between 1738 and 1750. The town's configuration was changing. In the past, St Paul's had been the central focus, with Westminster a royal and official area on the edge. Now the heart of the urban fabric extended between two bridges, from London Bridge, a little downriver from St Paul's, to Westminster Bridge, just downriver from the Abbey. And the time was approaching when the West End would itself become the centre.

This process did not mean, however, that the urban fabric immediately around the Abbey became denser; on the contrary, more space was opened out. This was probably due partly to changes of taste – people now set a higher value on Gothic architecture, and they liked to see major monuments clearly, without lesser buildings jammed round them – and partly to a concern to dignify the centre of national government and ceremony. The houses to the north of the Abbey were swept away. Though Broad Sanctuary remains as a name, it gradually lost its separate identity as demolitions extended northwards, eventually to form Parliament Square.

Regency taste is reflected in the text accompanying Ackermann's engravings of the Abbey in two folio volumes, published in 1812. The author is delighted that the houses by the church have gone, so that the eye can 'comprehend the grand impressive range' of the structure, regrets that nothing can be done to clear the jumble of buildings on the south side, and expresses the hope that St Margaret's Church, which 'ranges so ill' with the Abbey, should be taken away and rebuilt on another site. Some of these opinions may surprise us today, but they remind us that it is comparatively recent clearances which have brought about the present appearance of St Margaret's plumped neatly on a lawn in front of the larger church, as though the Abbey had laid an egg.

On 16 October 1834, a fire for the third time affected the Abbey's character, when most of the Palace of Westminster burned down. The new Houses of Parliament, by Barry and Pugin, changed the church's relationship to the city around it. Already in the eighteenth century the widening of St Margaret's Lane between Abbey and palace had loosened the fabric, and now the replacement of the curious jumble of buildings that had made up the old palace with one immense structure finally turned palace and Abbey into two separate monuments planted on either side of a road, rather than parts of an extended complex. However, the new structure showed a sensitivity to its context, echoing the panelling and even the design of the turrets on Henry VII's Chapel (this, one suspects, was Pugin's doing). This was a deliberate attempt to bind the two buildings together. Accidental, perhaps, is the felicitous view of four neo-Gothic towers that one can get from Victoria Street, south-west of the Abbey: the twin towers in the foreground, the tower of St Margaret's (by John James, who saw the twin towers to completion after Hawksmoor's death) to the left and beyond the improbable fantasy of the clock tower (Big Ben) – all towers which have, as it happens, a touch of playfulness to them, now with the insubstantial circle of the London Eye, spectral but festive, looming beyond. It is a prospect best enjoyed on a sunny day

22. Four of Westminster's neo-Gothic towers: the Abbey's twin towers, by Hawksmoor, 1735–45, the tower of St Margaret's (1735–7, by John James), and the nineteenth-century Clock Tower of the Houses of Parliament (Big Ben), by Barry and Pugin.

in winter, with the gilding sparkling on Big Ben; in summer the view is partially blocked by a tree in leaf.

But no longer was the Abbey the dominant accent in this part of London: the new palace was larger in extent, its towers much loftier, its exterior more richly decorated. Back in 1782, Karl Philipp Moritz, entering London across Westminster Bridge, had noted the two main accents on the skyline, 'the round, modern, majestic cathedral of St Paul's to the right' and on the left, in contrast, 'the long medieval pile of Westminster Abbey with its enormous pointed roof'. But now Hawthorne, heading for his first visit to the Abbey, found that he had passed it without noticing, because his eye had been drawn 'by the gaudier show of the new houses of Parliament'. But on reflection he decided that the earlier building won the competition: 'It is wonderful how the old weather-stained and smoke-blackened Abbey shames down this bran-newness.' Since then, time has changed the aesthetic balance yet again. The palace is no longer new, but has the patina of a century and a half of London life upon it, and it is the Abbey, cleaned and refaced, that looks spick and span.

The new Houses of Parliament effected a more permanent change in cutting the Abbey off from the river. For centuries artists had loved to paint it from the Thames; now that view was gone. The church still contrasted with the brick houses to its north, and towered above them until the turn of the century, when an enlarged Parliament Square was ringed with a sequence of very large monumental buildings in Portland stone: the Treasury, the Middlesex Guildhall and Methodist Central Hall. Westminster Abbey no longer soars above the secular life clustered at its foot: now it answers on the south of Parliament Square to the Treasury on the north – Church on one side, state on the other. Older accounts of the Abbey speak of its towering height; modern visitors sometimes express disappointment that it is not bigger. Internally, buildings usually look their actual size; externally, our sense of their size is greatly influenced by their surroundings. (St Patrick's Cathedral in New York is a striking example of this – a very large church which cannot help looking modest in scale on the outside.)

Parliament Square is a disappointing piece of urban space, and it is worth asking why. Trafalgar Square, also carved out by demolition, and surrounded by buildings of indifferent quality (except for St Martin-in-the-Fields), feels like a true urban node; its shape is fluid and dynamic, and it has now been transformed by the pedestrianisation of the north side, so that the National Gallery rises with a new and more spacious dignity from the public concourse. If it could be completely cleared of traffic, it might even pretend to be among the great piazzas of Europe. Parliament Square, with some great and more good architecture around it, merely seems to be a space between buildings. It is partly that its edges are not clearly defined; Whitehall, for instance, extended southwards in the mid-eighteenth century as Parliament Street, is too wide where it enters the square. And south-west of the Abbey London falls apart. When the Victorians drove Victoria Street through the slums of Westminster, they gave themselves a great opportunity, and they muffed it. They lined the street with drab, gloomy blocks; most of these were ripped down in the 1960s, to be replaced by slabs that were equally dreary in their own way – another chance missed. And so the Abbey has remained, oddly, on a frontier, and the legacy of its medieval situation, between London and the country, continues to affect the modern city. Other cities outclass London in aesthetic quality and monumental scale, but nowhere else so well expresses the idea that the business of government and administration is at the heart of national life. North of the Abbey, in Whitehall, bureaucracy seems almost glorious; to the south-west, you seem to have strayed into Bucharest.

London is a strange city, both old and not old. It has been continuously the most important city in the country to which it belongs for 2,000 years, and that cannot be said of any other place in Europe, not even Paris, and certainly not Rome. Yet it has preserved less of its past than most comparably old and large cities. Overwhelmingly, its fabric is nineteenth- and twentieth-century, even in the most historic areas. A few streets or districts preserve an eighteenth-century flavour, but domestic buildings earlier than 1700 are pretty few (in the City itself there is only one). The rebuilding after the Great Fire did away with most of the City's medieval churches, including the cathedral, Old St Paul's. So where antiquity pokes through in London, it tends to come unexpectedly – a scrawny stretch of Roman wall by the car park, or plum-red Queen Anne brick next to the concrete. Perhaps the most moving plunge into the past is offered by the church of St Bartholomew the Great. It looks unpromising outside, but to walk through the door is to step in an instant from the twenty-first century into the twelfth, so old is the place, so grey, so quiet. Westminster Abbey has a comparable effect. Outside it is almost part of an Edwardian ensemble, and much of its stonework is indeed newer than that of the buildings around it, while the porches are unmistakably Victorian; but pass inside, and you are startled to find yourself in such an old, lofty and un-English church, transported in a moment from London's prose to medieval poetry.

The contrast is not just between the outside of the church and its interior, but between the north side of the Abbey and the south. The southern end of Dean's Yard offers perhaps the best external view of the church, looming above a modest range of buildings which are an informal mixture of medieval and later centuries. This prospect still gives a good idea of how the Abbey looked from all sides in earlier times. It is surprising how humble and crumbly these old clerical houses are, their rough stone patched with brick, and their Georgian windows punctuating an older fabric with agreeable irregularity; it is almost as though we have been whisked in a twinkling from the middle of a metropolis into the cathedral close of a rural diocese. The notes of solitude and melancholy, echoing through earlier visitors' descriptions, usually seem remote from the Abbey's character today. Yet even now, especially in the winter months, the passages and little courtyards to the south of the cloister may still fit Washington Irving's picture of a region which retains the seclusion of former days and bears 'marks of the gradual dilapidations of time, which yet has something touching and pleasing in its very decay'. The secret world (or so it can seem) of Westminster Abbey offers a special and unusual kind of urban experience. In these quiet, carious areas, with their odd air of almost rustic neglect, are the oldest vestiges of the Abbey, as old as the eleventh century. To the south they open out into the unexpectedly spacious expanse of the Abbey garden, bounded on the east by a wall on the other side of which is the patch of grass where politicians are paraded to feed soundbites to the television cameras; only a skin of brick separates these two so different worlds.

Though London has kept less of its past than many great cities, it has preserved at Westminster an exceptional medieval group comprising not only the Abbey church and its ancillary buildings but also the surviving parts of the medieval Palace of Westminster, themselves more extensive than most people realise. It is an extraordinary fact that the most spectacular wooden roof ever constructed, in Westminster Hall, should be just across the street from the most spectacular stone roof, in Henry VII's Chapel. Westminster Hall is perhaps the finest medieval room in Europe, and redolent of history – here Charles I was tried and Warren Hastings impeached – and it is a shame that the people no longer have easy access to it. In the old days you could walk into Westminster Hall at any time of the day and, even in an age of heightened security, that ought surely still to be possible. We should be allowed to enjoy Westminster as a whole, Abbey and Hall together.

It is also something of a scandal that heavy traffic grinds and thunders between the Abbey and the Houses of Parliament, passing within a few feet of the end of Henry VII's Chapel. Mockingly, a section of this grim artery still officially bears the ancient name of Old Palace Yard. If the traffic could be eliminated or reduced, and the area redesigned, it ought to become possible to experience abbey and palace, once again, as complementary parts of a magnificent architectural complex. It is a pity that the houses to the west of Old Palace Yard and its continuation, Abingdon Street, have disappeared (some Georgian houses were demolished as recently as the 1960s, victims of an underground car park): the present patches of lawn and paving look arbitrary and embarrassed, more like the tidying up of an archaeological site than well-formed urban space. But a good landscape architect could surely transform this. For that matter, Parliament Square too, once freed from the traffic that now torments it, might appear rather impressive after all (at present there is a scheme to pedestrianise it, threatened by lack of funds). The Gothic complex of the Abbey and the Houses of Parliament and the Georgian, Victorian and Edwardian complex of Whitehall, if presented with more style and dignity, would together give London a very noble monumental centre. It could be done. All it needs is some money, some courage and some imagination.

8

THE NATION'S SHRINE

There is a part of Westminster Abbey's story which draws to a close sometime towards the end of the nineteenth century. It ceases to be the artistic force that it had been for more than 600 years. Funerary sculpture comes almost completely to an end, partly because such display went out of fashion, partly because there was no more room. It is not that the church was no longer a living and changing fabric. New stained glass has appeared throughout the twentieth century. Across a period of more than forty years a series of windows by the ecclesiastical architect and designer Ninian Comper was installed along the north aisle of the nave. Opinions about Comper differ: Betjeman adored him; Pevsner bit his tongue. His taste was refined, decorative, sumptuous, yet a little bloodless (asked about a cope he had designed for the Archbishop of Paris, he replied in his mannered accent, 'I simply *spettered* it with fleurs-de-lys'). One might have expected his style in stained glass to be too pallid for the Abbey, but it fits surprisingly well. After the Second World War the Abbey turned for glass to the technically skilful but painfully sentimental Hugh Easton. The newest addition is a window in Henry VII's Chapel, designed by Alan Younger and installed in 2000; the bottom right-hand corner depicts the donors, Lord and Lady Harris of Peckham, kneeling in medieval fashion. The work done inside the Abbey since the Second World War is to some extent a restoration, bringing its appearance back closer to what it had been in the sixteenth century, and yet one cannot quite escape the feeling that it reflects the taste of Stephen Dykes-Bower, who became surveyor of the fabric in 1951. It is a distinctive taste, a curious mixture of sensitive, prim and gaudy – not unlike Comper, but without his flair. Under Dykes-Bower the walls were cleaned, Victorian stained glass damaged by enemy action taken out and replaced by plain glass, the chandeliers of Waterford crystal installed. The very bright gilding and painting of the Elizabethan tombs suits their semi-barbarous splendour; the similar treatment of the pulpitum is garish. Dykes-Bower also devised the painted ceiling of the crossing, a design more Gothic Revival than Gothic.

Outside the church the craft of architectural sculpture lives on, in new corbels and decorative features and most recently in the pleasing statues of Christian martyrs of the twentieth century, placed above the west door in 1998. The official heritage bodies wanted this work to be given to well-known sculptors, but the Dean and Chapter insisted that it should be executed by the craftsmen who had worked on the building's restoration, and thus a medieval tradition was continued. In various forms, the patronage of art has continued at the Abbey across the past hundred years, and yet something has changed. What we see now is the honourable sustaining of some special and traditional skills, not the mainstream of the art of the age. And as it happens, the Abbey's taste was distinctly conservative throughout the twentieth century. Plenty of cathedrals and other churches have risked bolder stained glass, with results across the full range from disastrous to inspiring. Other churches contain sculpture by Henry Moore and Barbara Hepworth, but not the Abbey. Graham Sutherland and John Piper made works for other old churches, in glass, tapestry and paint, but not here. In fact, arts-and-crafts, art nouveau and modernism are all effectively unrepresented. There was some loss of nerve in this. A visitor from Mars might conclude that this aesthetic timidity corresponded to a lessening of the Abbey's significance, as it retreated gracefully into a decent role as repository of history and tradition. The Martian would be completely wrong. In fact, the twentieth century gave the Abbey a new political importance – political in the broad sense of influencing public sentiment, at home and abroad, but also, as we shall see, in terms of the party political scramble. This new story has its roots in the Victorian age.

In the second half of the nineteenth century St Paul's Cathedral became a high-church powerhouse, with R. W. Church, the historian of the Oxford Movement, as Dean and Henry Liddon, a preacher of thrilling power, as a canon. Westminster Abbey also began to draw large congregations, but by going in a different direction. Arthur Penrhyn Stanley, appointed Dean in 1864, was resolutely latitudinarian. It is he essentially who turned Westminster Abbey into a national church. On his deathbed, in 1881, he declared, 'I am yet humbly trustful that I have sustained before the life of the nation the extraordinary value of the Abbey as a religious, national and liberal institution.' All those adjectives bear weight: for the past century and a half, the Abbey has tried to balance the sometimes conflicting claims of nation, liberality and religion, and its history has been one of a continually broadening inclusiveness, in both religious and secular terms.

The Abbey had begun to show signs of a more inclusive approach to religious differences even in the early eighteenth century. The improbable catalyst was John Sheffield (1648-1721), first Duke of Buckingham of the second creation, amateur man of letters, patron of Dryden and friend of Pope. Pope was a Roman Catholic by birth, and Dryden had gone over to Rome during the brief reign of James II. When James was driven out and William and Mary assumed the throne, Dryden was stripped of the laureateship, but on his death, in 1700, the Dean, Thomas Sprat, secured his burial in the Abbey and he was interred with full ceremony. Later, Buckingham paid for a monument, not forgetting an inscription recording his generosity.

Although Buckingham, at least sometimes, indicated sympathy for Catholics, his own tomb seems to suggest that he sat lightly to religious dogma of any kind. We have already seen him smashing the royal monopoly on Henry VII's Chapel with his own monument and inscribing the cool, conditional character of his allegiance to the king upon it. The epitaph itself is even more striking:

Dubius, sed non improbus vixi. Incertus morior non perturbatus; Humanum est Nescire et Errare. Deo Confido Omnipotenti Benevolentissimo. Ens Entium Miserere mei.

(I lived doubtful but not dishonest. I die unsure but unafraid. It

is human not to know and to be in error. I trust in God, Almighty and all kindly. Being of beings, have mercy on me.)

The power of this comes from the flicker between a kind of Stoic pride and a kind of Christian humility. It is most dramatic at the end, where the philosophical abstraction of *'ens entium'*, 'being of beings', collides with the ancient words of the Mass, *'miserere mei'*. And thus Buckingham, who commemorated a papist within the walls of the Abbey, brings deism into it also. He enlarges its theology, as it were, in two quite different directions. But no doubt these things were more easily as well as more tersely said in the obscurity of a learned language.

It was not until Stanley, however, that the Abbey embraced ecumenism – as we should now say – as a definite mission. He was a passionate Liberal Anglican, following in the footsteps of his hero, Thomas Arnold, who had been headmaster of Rugby School when he was a boy there, and whose life he wrote. He drew huge congregations by inviting popular preachers of varied churchmanship, including freechurchmen and laymen, and he even allowed a Unitarian to receive communion, provoking widespread outrage. He also arranged some very popular burials (if one can call them that). This required diplomacy. The business of getting the dead into a national pantheon is, when one thinks about it, somewhat awkward. It is uncomfortable to offer a place in advance, and so usually a widow or children must make a rapid decision at a painful time. Local patriotism and family loyalty can get in the way too. Boswell opined that Dr Johnson's satisfaction at the prospect of burial in the Abbey was natural to any man of imagination, but the voice of the

Scottish laird is heard as he continues, 'who has no family sepulchre in which he can be laid with his fathers'. Dickens had wished to be buried at Rochester, but when he died suddenly in 1870, the press called for him to go to the Abbey, and Stanley managed the negotiation with his executor. One condition was that the time and place of the interment should be kept secret; the grave in the south transept was dug at night and the body was laid to rest the next morning. But the news got out and vast crowds thronged to see the coffin in the still-open grave; there had not been such a pilgrimage since the Middle Ages. 'Dickens is one of those writers who are well worth stealing,' George Orwell was to write. 'Even the burial of his body in Westminster Abbey was a species of theft, if you come to think of it.' But that was unfair. Stanley was not snatching the body for the establishment; he was responding to the public will and opening his church to embrace it. And thus, at least half by accident, the Abbey started on its new career as a site for popular ceremony and commemoration.

David Livingstone died upcountry in Africa, but Stanley secured him for the Abbey even so. His heart remained in the continent to which he gave his life, but the rest of him was carried to the coast, wrapped in bark and sailcloth, and transported to London. The burial of a Presbyterian missionary in this Anglican church was a significant act. Stanley himself was to be given a more sumptuous tomb than any Dean of Westminster, before or since. His funeral in 1881 prompted from Matthew Arnold a long ode, called simply *Westminster Abbey*; unluckily, it is one of his weakest performances. Disraeli had insisted that he should lie beside his wife at Hughenden; so there was no state funeral in the Abbey for

[153]

him, much to the Queen's disappointment. But seventeen years later Gladstone was buried there with full state honours, much to the Queen's disappointment. When Darwin died in 1882, the Abbey seemed the only possible place, and few people now thought his agnosticism a bar. He was 'the greatest Englishman since Newton', declared the *Pall Mall Gazette*, and the two men now lie side by side. His funeral was as magnificent as Newton's, too: the pall-bearers in the Abbey included not only Darwin's scientific collaborators, Wallace, Huxley and Hooker, but two dukes and an earl, the president of the Royal Society and the American ambassador. Yet this was, once more, against the wishes of the deceased: Darwin was devoted to his home at Downe in Kent, and had hoped to lie in the churchyard, beside his brother and his two dead babies, 'the sweetest place on earth', as he had once told a friend; but his widow felt that she must agree to the honour. His beloved dog Polly died a few days later. She at least was allowed to rest in the chalky downland soil, among the earthworms to which her master had devoted his last researches: Darwin's son buried her under the Kentish Beauty apple tree in the orchard.

⧗

Stanley was not himself much interested in enhancing the Abbey's furnishings or liturgy, but his deanship did see the Victorian age's chief work inside the church, the altar and reredos designed by Sir Gilbert Scott. His sermon at the altar's dedication shows both continuity with past tradition and an adaptation to the tone of the present time – a familiar combination in the Abbey:

*We, God's humble servants, entirely desire His fatherly goodness
to accept it as our oblation, our Easter offering. 'The earth is the
Lord's and the fullness thereof': everything that there is of beauty
in sculpture, poetry, painting or architecture, everything that
there is of skill in mechanical contrivance, has its religious side,
has the link, if it can be found, which binds it round the throne of
God and the gates of heaven. The alabaster from our Midland
quarries, the marble from our Cornish rocks, mosaic colours from
the isles of Venice, the porphyry from the shores of the Nile or of
the Bosphorus, the jewels from the far-off coasts of Asia and
America, combine as truly now in the service of Him who has
'given us the heathen for our possession, the uttermost parts of the
earth for our inheritance', as did the gold of Ophir and the san-
dulwood of India for the temple of Solomon.*

These sentences resonate with echoes from the Bible and the
Book of Common Prayer; consciously or not, they also echo
earlier accounts of the precious and exotic stones brought back
from Italy by Abbot Ware to make the pavement before the
altar. We have already heard Flete describing the 'stones of porphyry, jasper and marble of Thasos' acquired by Ware. In the
reign of Charles II Henry Keepe wonders at the pavement,
'where in most artificial work and delightful figures, you have
the Jasper, the Porphyry, the Lydian, the Touch, the Alabaster,
and the Serpentine stones'. Now, in the nineteenth century,
Scott had in turn inserted into the platform of his altar three
circles of Egyptian porphyry, brought back from the east by
Lord Elgin and presented to the Abbey by his grandson; a Latin
inscription records their provenance in ancient Byzantium.

The implication is of a great continuity across the centuries. But there has also been a change. The thirteenth-

century Abbey rose in an island kingdom on the edge of Christendom: the works of Henry III and Richard Ware are an attempt to connect to the centre, to sources of cultural or spiritual authority, to France and Rome. Stanley's rhetoric, by contrast, presents the Abbey as a central site to which the nations bring their tribute. It shares its worldwide panorama with some nineteenth-century hymnody – with Heber's survey stretching 'From Greenland's icy mountains' to India, Africa and Java, with C. E. Oakley's 'Hills of the North, rejoice', envisioning the Christianisation of the coral isles of the southern seas, of utmost east and west. Stanley was presumably aware that he was misquoting the second Psalm. 'Ask of me,' it reads 'and I *shall* give thee ... the uttermost parts of the earth for thine inheritance.' That promise, fantastical in ancient Israel, had apparently come true for Queen Victoria's Britain. And the new altar expressed this truth. High upon the screen, this text from the Book of Revelation is inscribed: 'The kingdoms of this world are become the kingdoms of our Lord and of his Christ.' The author of these words had envisaged a final apocalypse, but in this setting they seem to celebrate the spread of missionary endeavour in the empire's wake. The Abbey is remarkably free from nationalism, from 'frantic boast and foolish word' (to quote Kipling's warning poem *Recessional*, sung at the burial of the Unknown Warrior in 1920), but it could not altogether escape the imperial tinge.

Stanley's own outlook, nevertheless, was not so much imperial as international: though he described the Abbey as a national institution, he also wanted it to serve the English-speaking world as a whole. Evidently he had an 'American policy', and it is telling that Trinity Church, Boston's unofficial cathedral, where he had preached, erected a bust in his memory. Americans have from time to time claimed a stake in the Abbey. Daniel Webster is said to have burst into tears on entering it, and Hawthorne declared, 'An American has a right to be proud of Westminster Abbey; for most of the men who sleep in it, are our great men, as well as theirs.' That sentiment comes from a time when white America was still largely British in ancestry, and also from a period when those Americans who wanted to give their nation historic depth needed more than now to look outside its borders. But the Abbey's American connection goes back to the colonial era. Hawthorne decided that Sir Peter Warren (who died in 1752) owed his place there to the valour of the New Englanders who took Louisburg under his command. (Warren's American wife had paid for his monument, by Roubiliac.) The Province of Massachusetts put up a monument to Lord Howe, who had been killed on an expedition to Ticonderoga in 1758; it is interesting to see this display of loyalty, grander than anything the colonists erected on their own soil, so few years before the Boston Tea Party, and from puritan New England, not an Anglican colony such as Virginia.

Hawthorne was disappointed that he could find only one grave of a native American (his term), and that this was William Wragg, who acquired his memorial 'by the most un-American of qualities, his loyalty to his king' – a dubious judgement historically, but an early example of the concept of un-American activity. Wragg was drowned sailing from South Carolina to England in 1777; there is a poignant epitaph. Next to him is the memorial to Major André, hanged as a spy by Washington, who had refused both the calls for clemency from his own side and the victim's own plea for an honourable death by firing squad. This incident stirred passions back home. Anna Seward wrote:

> O Washington! I thought thee great and good,
> Nor knew thy Nero-thirst for guiltless blood,
> Severe to use the power that fortune gave,
> Thou cool, determined murderer of the brave.

The monument, by contrast, shows the uses of understatement: a graceful relief depicts Washington refusing clemency, André being led to execution, and two mourning figures said to represent Innocence and Mercy; there is no overt criticism in word or image, the inscription actually declaring that he was 'lamented even by his foes'. The story has a sequel. In 1879 a memorial was erected at the place where André died; the inscription records that his remains had been removed to Westminster Abbey, and goes on to celebrate 'those better feelings which have since united two nations one in race in language and in religion with the hope that this friendly union will never be broken'. The inscription ends with the name of its author: 'Arthur Penrhyn Stanley, Dean of Westminster'. Washington is also quoted on the monument, paying tribute to the man he had put to death. So the story ends with reconciliation (with perhaps a touch of anxious exculpation thrown in).

By Stanley's time, other things were changing too. In Hawthorne's day, while Americans might claim the Abbey as part of their heritage, that feeling is not yet echoed by the place itself. But as the United States grows more powerful and as immigration from continental Europe starts to transform it, the British become more interested in affirming the bonds between the English-speaking peoples. We can read this story on the Abbey's walls. In 1884 Longfellow is honoured in the south transept, the inscription declaring, 'This bust was placed among the memorials of the poets of England by the English admirers of an American poet'. Conversely, stained-glass windows commemorating George Herbert and William Cowper had been installed in 1875, with a Latin inscription recording that the donor was 'George William Childs, American Citizen'. When James Russell Lowell, minor man of letters and former American minister in London, died in 1891, a tablet in his memory, with a portrait head, was set up at the entrance to the chapter house 'by his English friends'. It was to be joined by a plaque to Walter Hines Page, American ambassador during the First World War, 'friend of Great Britain in her sorest need'. A sorer need was to come; and American support in the Second World War is remembered in the memorial to Franklin D. Roosevelt, conspicuously placed at the west end of the nave, facing the Unknown Warrior, and 'erected by the Government of the United Kingdom'.

We have seen how often Westminster Abbey has looked abroad, especially to the aesthetic or spiritual authority of France and Italy. England was on Europe's periphery, and it looked to the Continent as to a centre. But in time Britain itself became central, and the Abbey a source of authority for others. The National Cathedral in Washington, DC, is the most conspicuous attempt to create a Westminster Abbey across the sea, within the limits possible in a country where Church and state are separate and Episcopalians a small minority. In design, it aims to be the perfect Gothic cathedral; in function, to act as a spiritual focus for the whole nation. Like the Abbey, it looks abroad for its inspiration, though now to England itself, and to a lesser extent France. One of the original architects, G. F. Bodley, was British, bringing his English experience to Washington, as Henry of Reynes had once brought French experience to Westminster. And as Henry of Reynes brought the forms of Rheims and the Sainte-Chapelle to London, so the National Cathedral patterns itself upon Canterbury and Lincoln: the proportions and modelling of its three towers owe a particular debt to Canterbury, while Lincoln (another three-towered church) is evoked by the hill-top site and the giant niche on the west front. Inside, the design of the gallery is especially close to Westminster; the most obviously French feature is the apsidal east end, but this, of course, is also the Abbey's form. Richard Ware had once brought marbles from Rome to make the sanctuary floor; the National Cathedral, for its part, incorporates stone from Canterbury Cathedral, mother church of the Anglican Communion, in the pulpit, and stone from Glastonbury, Whitby and Iona elsewhere. Royal tombs are impossible in a republic – or are they? Woodrow Wilson is honoured with a stone sarcophagus beneath a canopy, not unlike the Plantagenets at Westminster, and perhaps that speaks a kind of truth, for the Founding Fathers developed their idea of the presidency from the place of the king in the British constitution. One is tempted to say that, unlike Britain, the USA remains a constitutional monarchy, perhaps the only true constitutional monarchy in the world.

The National Cathedral is very handsome, but no one would claim that it rivals the Abbey's hold on the affections of its country. We might apply to it Hawthorne's words – grey, light, cold, fresh and new, stately; but these are the terms that he applied to St Paul's, contrasting it with the Abbey. Whereas the Abbey is a mighty sympathiser, the National Cathedral sits aloof above the urban sprawl, at a distance from its centre. It is in the wrong place, and perhaps it is in the wrong city – in the administrative capital, not at the nation's heart. London is a coalescence of functions, the administrative, cultural, financial and commercial capital of a large nation – as are Paris and Cairo, and few other cities in the world. The Abbey likewise is a jumbled coalescence of functions, and it is now, as it was not originally, at the heart of its city. Here too many styles and centuries fuse or collide. It succeeds as a 'national cathedral' because it has itself been like a nation, living in time, changing but continuous, battered, worn, restored. It succeeds also because it is not so much national as natural, its functions having developed without much conscious design; it is fitting that the high priest of evolutionary theory should be buried within its walls.

9

THE SITE OF CEREMONY

Every English monarch since William the Conqueror has been crowned in Westminster Abbey, except for Edward V and Edward VIII, the two who were never crowned at all. The English coronation ceremony has several parts: the Recognition, deriving from the acclamation of Frankish and Anglo-Saxon kings; the Oath, symbolising the contract between monarch and people; the Crowning, which is Roman in origin; the Anointing, based on the Old Testament, by which the Church consecrates the sovereign; and the homage of the Lords Spiritual and Temporal (but not of the Commons), a survival of feudal practice. In its essentials this series of rituals goes back to Anglo-Saxon times and is more than a thousand years old. Yet some historians and sociologists see the British coronation as an example of 'the invention of tradition', arguing that its meaning has constantly changed and that the dazzling pageant with which we are familiar is largely a modern creation, hardly more than a hundred years old. How far is this true?

Time after time, to be sure, a coronation has brought some innovation, or had a character distinctive to itself. Before his crowning, Richard II processed through the city

23. The crowning of James II, 1685. Although James was Britain's last Roman Catholic king, the ceremony was Anglican, and the prelates are robed with Protestant sobriety.

from the Tower of London at its eastern edge to Westminster, a custom then followed by his successors up to Charles II. Edward VI was the first Protestant to be crowned, and the first to be crowned by a Church which he governed. Mary I refused to be crowned on the Coronation Chair, because her heretic brother had sat there. Elizabeth I's was the first coronation to be conducted in English; she is said to have asserted her no-nonsense Protestantism by complaining that the oil for her anointing smelled bad. The Archbishop of Canterbury refused to crown her, and she had to make do with the Bishop of Carlisle instead. James I's coronation united the crowns of England and Scotland. Charles II's coronation marked a restoration after more than a decade of republican government. James II, as a Roman Catholic, refused to receive Communion from an Anglican prelate, and so that part of the service had to be curtailed. William and Mary's was, uniquely, a double monarchy; William took the Coronation Chair, and a second chair had to be built for his wife's crowning. George I was a foreigner who did not speak English. George II's crowning was ennobled by Handel's Coronation Anthems; the most famous of them, 'Zadok the Priest', has accompanied the anointing at every coronation since. At George III's coronation the Earl Marshal's deputy apologised to the King for various botches, adding with a fine absence of diplomacy that he had arranged for everything to go right next time. That next time was not to come for sixty years, when George IV spent unprecedented sums on the event: he even had Wren's altarpiece taken down, so that more tiers of seating could be installed at the east end. But the splendour was marred by ugly and pathetic farce, as Caroline, his estranged queen, barred from the ceremony, struggled to get in through the Abbey's locked doors and turned away in tears. William IV, by contrast, disliked ceremonial and only agreed under protest to be crowned at all; even so, he managed to get the service cut down so much that it was nicknamed the Half-Crownation (a play on the half-crown coin). Victoria's coronation was notoriously unsatisfactory; the music was poorly sung, the clergy got in a muddle, an elderly peer fell when performing his act of homage, and the Archbishop of Canterbury forced the Queen's ring painfully on to the wrong finger.

For all that, we can make too much of the muddle at earlier coronations. Most people, clearly, found them very impressive. 'What is the finest sight in the world? A Coronation,' wrote Horace Walpole after attending George III's, even though he regarded the ritual itself as hocus-pocus. Victoria's coronation looks wonderful in the many paintings and engravings of it. Of course, these pictures may romanticise the scene, but it is interesting to find at least one that shows the young queen helping the stumbling peer to his feet. That was felt as a charming, human touch, not (as it would be today) an embarrassing fluff in a performance of almost military precision. The fact is that broadcasting and recording have changed the character of public ceremonial: when every detail can be both seen and revisited by millions, a formality and exactness are required which earlier ages did not look for. 'Worship is the opera of elevated, serious and believing souls,' said Hippolyte Taine, after attending a service at the Abbey in 1862, and a royal consecration is now opera produced to the highest international standard. We rehearse everything; our ancestors would have thought rehearsal to be somehow improper. Horace Walpole's famous account of the funeral of George II, the last king to be buried in the Abbey, is partly comic – a blundering bishop, a buffoonish duke, the congregation sitting or standing where they could, without solemnity or decorum – but he was also moved:

> *The charm was the entrance to the Abbey where we were received by the Dean and Chapter in rich copes, the choir and almsmen all bearing torches; the whole Abbey so illuminated that one saw it to greater advantage than by day, the tombs, long aisles and fretted roof all appearing distinctly and with the happiest chiaroscuro. There wanted nothing but incense and little chapels here and there with priests saying mass for the repose of the defunct – yet one could not complain of its not being catholic enough.*

Walpole speaks as a harbinger of romantic taste, but his words also indicate how evocative an ecclesiastical occasion could be even in the eighteenth century, and how suggestive of Catholicism and the Middle Ages, at a time when official Anglicanism is thought of as dry. He foreshadows the ritualism of the Victorian age as well as its enthusiasm for the Gothic.

None the less, a new sumptuousness appears in the ceremonies of the later nineteenth century. Queen Victoria's Golden Jubilee in 1887 can probably be reckoned the first modern celebration of royalty, inaugurating that sequence of magnificently staged, immensely popular festivals of joy and sometimes grief that would become part of the public life of twentieth-century Britain. At the service of thanksgiving the Queen sat not on a throne but on the Coronation Chair; she remains the only monarch to have occupied it twice. Her diary records the occasion in characteristic style:

I sat alone (oh! Without my beloved husband for whom this would have been such a proud day!) where I sat forty-nine years ago and received the homage of the Princes and the Peers, but in the Old Coronation Chair of Edward I, with the old stone brought from Scotland, on which the old Kings of Scotland used to be crowned.

My robes were beautifully draped in the chair. The service was very well done and arranged. The Te Deum by my darling Albert sounded beautiful, and the anthem by Dr. Bridge was fine, especially the way in which the National Anthem and dear Albert's Chorale were worked in.

We catch some of the touches that made Victoria's prose such a gift to parodists. But she was always a mixture of silliness and remarkably good sense, and along with her tiresomeness there are flashes of keen perception. She manages to turn a great national commemoration into a domestic anniversary (dear Albert is of course recurrent). But in a way she was right; unconsciously she echoes Bagehot's idea of how to be a modern monarch: 'a family on the throne is an interesting idea'. And she has the historical imagination to appreciate the double character of her seat – Edward's chair, Scotland's stone.

The Golden Jubilee was a fairly modest affair: the authorities had been unsure whether it would command popular support. But, not for the first or last time, the Abbey became the victim of its own success. The Diamond Jubilee, ten years later, was an enormous imperial celebration, assembling troops and potentates from across the globe, and for the pomp and circumstance of such a vast event, St Paul's Cathedral was required. But this occasion became, in effect, a rehearsal for the coronation of Edward VII in 1902, when the Abbey came back into its own. This was the first imperial coronation, not only because no previous monarch had come to his crowning as Emperor of India, but also because, as at the Diamond Jubilee, the capital was thronged with picturesque subjects from around the globe: Dyaks, Maoris, Chinese and, above all, Indians. The displays of native soldiery belonged, however, to the external life of London; within the Abbey, the service remained purely Anglican. Edward was also the first to be crowned as sovereign of British but independent dominions separated by thousands of miles from the motherland: Canada and Australia.

According to the press, this coronation was a superb spectacle. The music was excellently performed, and for the first time since the coronation of George II there were new works commissioned for the occasion which possessed genuine distinction and staying power. Psalm 122, 'I was glad when they said unto me', has been sung at the entrance of the monarch at every coronation since Charles I's. It has been sung in Parry's setting at every coronation since Edward VII's. Like Handel's 'Zadok the Priest', it has become part of the institution, another instance of old but evolving tradition.

But Edward's coronation was not without anxieties, large and small. The King had been struck down with appendicitis and, though passionately determined not to postpone the ceremony, was forced to agree when his doctors warned him that if he persisted, he might drop dead during the service. (It is an odd thought that, if the worst had happened, he would not have been the first king to die in the Abbey: Henry IV had already done it five centuries before.) The Bishop of Stepney, Cosmo Lang, declared that the nation had been approaching the event with undue levity and the postponement was a call to remember God. The Bishop of London said that the coronation had become 'too much a great show' and 'too little a great sacrament'. This idea that the events in the Abbey were a collective religious experience for the whole nation struck a new note. But it was also a social occasion: the sovereign arranged a special pew for a few of his lady friends, which some wag nicknamed 'the King's loose box'.

The King was still weak enough at the postponed ceremony for it to be shortened. The aged Archbishop of Canterbury, Frederick Temple, only a few months from death, tremulous and half-blind, had difficulty reading the service and lifting the crown, which the King had to adjust for him. By the time of the Communion he was in a state of such decrepitude that the King was said to be looking 'frightfully nervous'. The protagonists in this ceremony must have resembled the Emperor of China in *Turandot*, ancient, weary, pale and hieratic, and the more venerable for his frailty. And thus the special character of this coronation was the blend of ceremonial magnificence with human weakness. The illustrated papers made much of two unexpected gestures: the King kissing his son, and helping to his feet the Archbishop, after he had knelt for the oath of loyalty. It took the monarch and three prelates to get him up. The Bishop of Winchester offered sal volatile; 'Go away!' the Archbishop snapped.

George V's coronation (1911) was the first to be photographed (a few pictures were permitted); George VI's was the first to be filmed and broadcast on the radio; Elizabeth II's was the first to be televised. Only the anointing, the most sacred part of the ceremony, has remained private and unseen. And thus by degrees the coronation was opened to the people's view to an extent that had hardly been known since the Middle Ages. The medieval style of coronation lingered on at least into the sixteenth century, and is captured in the picture of Anne Boleyn's crowning in Shakespeare's *Henry VIII* (the author of the passage may be Shakespeare's collaborator Fletcher). A gentleman, asked where he has got so sweaty, explains:

> Among the crowd i'th'Abbey, where a finger
> Could not be wedged in more. I am stifled
> With the mere rankness of their joy.

He then describes the stream of lords and ladies escorting the Queen to a chair of state in the choir:

> Believe me, sir, she is the goodliest woman
> That ever lay by man; which when the people
> Had the full view of, such a noise arose
> As the shrouds make at sea in a stiff tempest,
> As loud and to as many tunes. Hats, cloaks –
> Doublets, I think – flew up, and had their faces
> Been loose, this day they had been lost. Such joy
> I never saw before.

Then the Queen kneels, saint-like, by the altar, rises again and bows to the people:

When by the Archbishop of Canterbury
　　She had all the royal makings of a queen,
　　As holy oil, Edward Confessor's crown
The rod and bird of peace, and all such emblems
Laid nobly on her. Which performed, the choir,
　　With all the choicest music of the kingdom,
Together sung *Te Deum*. So she parted,
And with the same full state paced back again
　　To York Place, where the feast is held.

This describes the crowning of a consort, not of a sovereign, and it is an imaginative reconstruction, eighty years after the event, but in essence it is probably authentic enough. The combination of sacrament and football crowd within one space is alien to our experience, but what unites past and present is the idea of coronation as a mass spectacle, and the sense of the religious consecration as the central part of a larger, secular festivity: the Abbey and the acts of dedication come in the middle of a description which begins with lords and ladies and ends with a slap-up meal.

Through royal occasions Westminster Abbey has become known across the globe, yet its widest influence on the world has come from something that is not royal at all. The idea of burying an unidentified soldier killed in the Great War came from David Railton, who had served as a chaplain on the western front, and was eagerly taken up by the Dean. And so, on 11 November 1920, the body of the Unknown Warrior was laid in the nave and the grave filled with a hundred bags of soil brought from the battlefield. The King, as chief mourner, scattered a handful of French earth upon the coffin – some corner of a foreign field that would indeed be forever

England. France had inspired the building of the Abbey, and now the substance of France lay within it. The grave was kept open for a week, and one and a quarter million people filed past in homage.

The inscription on the tomb ends, 'They buried him among the kings because he had done good toward God and toward his house.' These words are adapted from a biblical verse about a high priest who had supervised the restoration of the temple at Jerusalem. The text hardly fits the circumstances of the Great War, and yet it is oddly effective. Implicitly, it notes the significance of where the soldier lies; it connects the body and the building. The idea was inspired; the execution was, in some ways, clumsy. The lettering of the inscription is remarkably undistinguished. The tomb blocks the path to the west door. As you walk around the church, you tread upon the names of the obscure and the great – you can hardly avoid it; but no one walks on the Unknown Warrior. And so every procession, however solemn, must veer awkwardly to one side as it passes.

And yet these botches have acquired their own eloquence. The pain of war properly interrupts the smoothness of pageantry. And the commonplace lettering is humanising in its ordinariness, the sort of thing that you might find on the grave of your own loved one. A writer in the *British Legion Journal* tried to explain how the tomb in the Abbey related to the Cenotaph, the empty tomb, in Whitehall. The Cenotaph, he said, represents the noble army of the dead as a whole, whereas the Unknown Warrior 'represents one individual and the mystery as to whose son he was makes him the son and brother of us all. The Cenotaph, it may be said, is the token of our memory as a nation: the Grave of the Unknown

Warrior is the token of our memory as individuals.' Here, once more, the Abbey acts as a mighty sympathiser, a site for personal as well as collective memory.

The Tomb of the Unknown Warrior has been imitated all over the world, but the imitators have missed most of the point. The warrior at Westminster is 'buried among the kings', everyman among the mighty. Elsewhere, the unknowns are usually buried in isolated grandeur, militarised (often guarded by sentries), surrounded by arches of triumph or other apparatus of chauvinism (especially in those countries which have actually suffered defeat) – the 'frantic boast' from which the congregation attending the burial at Westminster prayed to be delivered. The French unknown lies under the Arc de Triomphe, that superbly mendacious commemoration of the war that Napoleon lost, the Italian unknown below the swagger of the Victor Emmanuel monument. The American unknown lies in Arlington National Cemetery; the site is fitting enough, but here the decision was made to have a series of unknowns, one for each major conflict, disastrously diluting the symbolism of the one man who stands for all. The unknown at Westminster is the only one of these warriors to be buried in a living, working church; in one sense singled out, in another he is joined to the universal rituals and consolations of death and mourning (almost it seems a pity that he should not be walked upon and bear the erosions of time, like everyone else). And so here, where the Abbey has been most imitated, it has proved inimitable after all.

In the twentieth century the Abbey has both measured the

royal family's popularity and helped to enhance it. Traditionally, the sovereign's children were married in the Chapel Royal or at Windsor, but in 1922 Princess Mary's wedding was held at Westminster, on a grand scale. The experiment was a success – a 'People's Wedding', one newspaper called it – and next year the Duke of York became the first prince of the royal house to be married in the Abbey since the Middle Ages. As the bridal couple left the church, the new Duchess, showing the flair which would serve her so well as Queen and Queen Mother, laid her wreath on the Unknown Warrior's grave. The Abbey now became the established place for royal weddings, until it once more fell victim to its own success, when the wedding which attracted the greatest worldwide interest of any in history, that of Charles and Diana, was moved to the larger St Paul's (one unlucky manufacturer of souvenirs had already printed the Abbey's towers on his offerings). Conversely, a decline in the royal family's collective popularity and the uncertainty that now attends their marriages led to the most recent wedding, that of the Earl and Countess of Wessex, being held in the comparative privacy of St George's Chapel, Windsor. In each case, the shift to or from the Abbey acted, positively or negatively, as a barometer of public affection.

In 1937 Cosmo Lang, now Archbishop of Canterbury, saw a new opportunity for evangelism in George VI's coronation, which would for the first time be heard live in Britain and across the world. (The use of microphones, incidentally, meant also that this was the first coronation audible to most of the congregation in the church itself.) In a broadcast talk he called for a 'beginning of the return of the nation to God', so that the King should not 'come alone to his hallowing'.

The service was more inclusive than before: for the first time representatives of the free churches were included in the procession and seated in the theatre around the King. Under the recent Statute of Westminster the King was now sovereign of each of his dominions separately (King of New Zealand, of South Africa, and so on) instead of 'ruler of the British Dominions across the sea'. Lang at first wanted to crown the King only as the British monarch, but the dominions were keen not to be left out and the oath had to be reworded. The pledge to uphold the Protestant religion as by law established then caused difficulty, above all in Ireland, but also in Canada and Australia; again some diplomatic adjustment was required.

Lang was also exercised by obscurer matters, like the place of the litany in the service and the restoration of an older form of anointing, 'rising from the hands to the head, instead of descending from the head to the hands. This also, I am sure, proved itself to be right.' The significance of this detail is opaque; but many agreed with Lang that the anointing was the most powerfully moving part of the service – the monarch stripped of his outer robes and clad only in white, kneeling for the Archbishop's blessing, the sanctity of the occasion enhanced by the King's evident sense of dedication and the electrifying sounds of 'Zadok the Priest'. Everything else in the coronation is ritual; this, unmistakably, is sacrament. The moment is both public and personal, intimate and universal; a canopy is held over the monarch to mask this private act, and no camera records it. The coronation service is a sacred space within a larger celebration, as Westminster Abbey is a sacred space within the larger city; and the anointing is especially sacred within the coronation service as the

24. Elizabeth II on the Coronation Chair after her crowning, 2 June 1953.
The chair is thirteenth-century and the rituals even older, but the 'almost
Byzantine magnificence' admired by Cecil Beaton is comparatively modern.
Contrast James II's coronation, on p 163.

shrine is especially sacred within the Abbey, national, central, but also hidden and strange.

For the diarist Chips Channon, on the other hand, the loveliest moment of all was 'the swirl when the Peeresses put on their coronets: a thousand white gloved arms, sparkling with jewels, lifting their tiny coronets' – and one would indeed be giving an incomplete picture of the occasion if one left out the fact that it was, among other things, the most brilliant event of the social calendar. Before Elizabeth II's coronation, Chips recorded that people talked about nothing except who were and were not 'Abbey happy' – in other words, who had been invited. He added a story about one divorced peer who had expressed to the Earl Marshal his fear that he would be ineligible to attend, only to be told, 'Of course you will; this is the Coronation, not Ascot.' Some observers thought that there were too many aristocrats in the congregation, and that more space might have been given to the Commonwealth. As Queen of Pakistan and of Ceylon, Elizabeth was the first British monarch to be crowned as sovereign of countries that were overwhelmingly non-Christian, but only minimal concessions were made to this new reality. The free churches were given a slightly larger role, and the Moderator of the Church of Scotland read a lesson.

This was the last imperial coronation. But its special character came from the time and from the person of the sovereign herself. After the years of austerity that had followed the war, people longed to celebrate, and the young Queen seemed a symbol of new hope. Archbishop Fisher, in sermons before the event, had stressed the burden of kingship and the symbolic weight of the crown. The Queen appeared for her anointing, unlike the kings, with her arms bare, and this, together with her youth, enhanced the sense of sacrificial vulnerability. It is fascinating to hear the camp tone of Cecil Beaton's diary yielding, in the end, to the occasion's splendour:

> *The cheeks are sugar-pink: her hair tightly curled around the Victorian diadem of precious stones straight on her brow. Her pink hands are folded meekly on the elaborate grandeur of her encrusted skirt; she is still a young girl with a demeanour of simplicity and humility. Perhaps her mother has taught her never to use a superfluous gesture. As she walks she allows her heavy skirt to swing backwards and forwards in a beautiful rhythmic effect. This girlish figure has enormous dignity; she belongs in this scene of almost Byzantine magnificence.*

It is ironic that what strikes Beaton as Byzantine — the prelates in their gold-encrusted copes — was a twentieth-century restoration which would have seemed impossibly Romish when Victoria was crowned. Chips Channon at George VI's coronation had thought of Renaissance Venice. Both men's imaginations are carried far away in time and place by the exoticism of this uniquely British occasion.

So is the coronation ceremony an example of the invention of tradition? Has its meaning constantly changed? If the meaning of an event is taken to inhere in what people think about it, there may be as many meanings as observers. Here is one. I was four years old at the last coronation. It is the earliest public event that I remember, and my first trip to a cinema was to see it on film. I also recall sitting on a low stone wall and watching a loyal procession of decorated vans and lorries coming up the village high street. What the coronation itself meant, I suppose, was a golden coach, a glittering crown and a beautiful queen. Of course queens were beautiful, like princesses in fairy stories. I had no sense of the Coronation as a religious occasion, and I doubt whether I felt it as patriotic either. Rather, it seemed to be a communal and collective event, not that I could have used those words; it was one of the things people did, and everyone joined in. I intrude these memories not because they have any importance, but to make the point that the meaning of an event, in this sense of 'meaning', is so unstable, varying so readily from person to person, that it is not in itself deeply significant. As time goes by, it will alter for the same person. Fifty years on, I now notice how hieratic and sacramental the coronation is, and how central is the act of anointing. And I am of course struck, as a small child could not be, by how young the Queen was.

There is another reason why each coronation has its own quality. A coronation is not only a public ceremony but also the initiation of an individual, and the person of the monarch affects its character. A republican country can appoint its head of state (too often a retired professor of economics), but a consequence of having a hereditary head of state is that you cannot choose what you get. The monarch may be admired or disliked. For most of the past two centuries, the British head of state has been a woman; that would not have happened under an elective system. Youth, a group otherwise kept out of high public office, also gets a chance of representation. But none of these changes of tone or character is fundamental. Sociologists and historians debate whether such ceremonies are forms of propaganda by which the ruling classes bolster their authority or means by which communities as a whole articulate and reaffirm popular values. Actually, the coronation is intrinsically neither of these things (whatever its effect may be): a coronation is something which is done because it always has been done. Part of its power, indeed, lies in its autonomy: it is death, not governments, that determines when a crowning is due.

Its power lies also in people's perception, however little articulated, however vaguely felt, that a fundamental meaning is embedded in the act itself – that there is a permanent presence at the heart of this ritual. And it is indeed very ancient. Consider the words with which the Queen was anointed:

> *Be thy Head anointed with holy Oil: as kings, priests, and prophets were anointed. And as Solomon was anointed King by Zadok the priest and Nathan the prophet, so be thou anointed, blessed and consecrated Queen over the Peoples, whom the Lord thy God hath given thee to rule and govern …*

Perhaps the most extraordinary thing about these extraordinary words is that they are true: in all probability Zadok did anoint Solomon as Geoffrey Fisher anointed Elizabeth II. This is the oldest of all Christian rituals, a thousand years older than Christianity itself. Or if that seems too fanciful, it is certain that while the nature of kingship has changed utterly, the main elements of the English coronation ritual have existed, essentially unchanged, for more than a millennium. The coronation is like the building in which it is enacted: the Abbey's exterior has hardly a medieval stone left, its interior has been constantly altered, its theology transformed, but it is still the same church and fundamentally it is still doing the same work.

The next coronation, like its predecessors, will have its own character and bring its own innovations. Most probably, the new king will be an elderly man, bruised by time and circumstance. The length and quality of the present Queen's old age will have affected public feeling about the monarchy in ways that cannot yet be predicted. The event will take place in a transformed setting: London, once regarded as concentrated essence of Britishness, is now more multiracial and multicultural than the country as a whole, and is bound to become even more so. We can be sure that the Roman Catholic Church, as well as the free churches, will be given a larger part, and that other faiths will have official representation. The peerage may lose its special role. There are other obvious speculations. But the likelihood is that the essence of the coronation will remain, not much watered down. And certainly the Abbey's history has suggested that becoming more 'high church' in liturgical style and becoming more inclusive are not contradictory tendencies. The immense appeal of the twentieth-century coronations owed much to the mystery and wonder at their centre, to the very fact that they were not the bland results of a search to locate the highest common factor among different beliefs and unbeliefs. And recent experience suggests that big royal occasions continue even now to be more popular than most people have expected beforehand.

Coronations and the commemoration of the Unknown

Warrior are political in a broad sense: they are acts of man as a social animal. It is a surprise, however, that the Abbey should have become significant at the end of the twentieth century in a more narrowly political way: each of the last two prime ministers has tried to use it for party advantage. The first of them was John Major, who in 1996 returned the Stone of Scone to Scotland.

The Stone of Scone is the seat on which the Scottish kings were crowned, before it was seized by Edward I in 1296 and brought to Westminster. Some have believed that it is in fact the Stone of Destiny once used at the coronation of the high kings of Ireland, but almost certainly it originated as a Scottish imitation of an Irish symbol. Legend held that it was the stone which Jacob used as his pillow when he dreamt his vision of the angels, as explained in some Latin verses formerly displayed in the Abbey, but Addison's Sir Roger de Coverley was not convinced (what evidence was there, he asked, that Jacob had ever been in Scotland?), nor has modern scientific geology been supportive. Edward I had the Coronation Chair made to hold the stone, it being fitted underneath the seat, and the English kings were thenceforth crowned upon it. But its significance was transformed in 1603 when James VI of Scotland was crowned first King of Great Britain, and it became an emblem of union. One might compare the unconscious symbolism of the words 'Scottorum Malleus', Hammer of the Scots, painted on Edward I's tomb in the sixteenth century, and now faded almost to oblivion. For Dean Stanley the chair and stone were 'the one primeval monument which binds together the whole empire'. So potent was the stone felt to be that when the Abbey's movable furnishings, including the Coronation

Chair, were taken to the country for safety during the Second World War, it stayed behind, buried in a secret place.

Major's government, unpopular throughout the country, was in especial difficulty north of the border, because of its opposition to devolution. The return of the stone, an idea which seems to have originated with the Secretary of State for Scotland, Michael Forsyth, was a clumsy attempt to buy public favour. The business was carried out furtively. Major first got the Queen's agreement (presumably she felt that she had to accept her chief minister's advice), and the Dean of Westminster was informed only two days before Major announced the decision to the House of Commons. Historic Scotland, the heritage body, was instructed, impossibly, to remove the stone from Westminster in secrecy and arrange for it to reach Scotland in a blaze of publicity. In the event, the press was present in force when the stone was removed by night. Like the sword in another stone, it refused to budge from the chair, and it took some hours to work it free. A senior officer of Historic Scotland signed, in triplicate, for the receipt of one sacred stone. The Dean and Chapter gathered grim-faced, in black cloaks, to register their unspoken opinion of what was done.

When Major announced the stone's return to Scotland, the obvious question took him by surprise: where in Scotland? He seems to have assumed that Edinburgh Castle would be the place, but some gestures of public consultation were hurriedly arranged. St Giles's Cathedral was one suggestion, Scone Palace another. In the end the stone did go to Edinburgh Castle. The government did not want to spend money on its gesture, however, and since the castle was being splendidly refurbished anyway, the stone could be housed there with hardly any additional expense. And so now it sits on velvet in a glass case, alongside the Honours of Scotland (the Scottish crown jewels). It looks absurd, and the Honours of Scotland look embarrassed beside it. The trouble is that as far as physical appearance goes, the Stone is only a stone. Back in the eighteenth century Goldsmith's Chinese Citizen of the World could see no point in it: if he could have beheld Jacob's head on Jacob's pillow, that would have been a curious sight, 'but in the present case, there was no more reason for my surprise than if I should pick a stone from their streets, and call it a curiosity, merely because one of their kings happened to tread upon it as he passed in a procession'. All its potency lies in history, association and sanctity; shorn of its mana, imprisoned behind a vitrine in a museum, it appears meaningless. One would have to be pretty unimaginative to believe that Scotland has been honoured by this.

Displays of weakness do not win votes, and at the subsequent election, to the detriment of British democracy, the Conservatives lost every seat in Scotland; so in party terms, Major's gesture failed entirely. Since the Coronation Chair was made to hold the stone, its removal was, in antiquarian and aesthetic terms, the mutilation of a rare and powerfully eloquent medieval artefact. The hollow space under the seat of the chair looks simply wrong. Statesmen are said to think anxiously about what history will say of them; their weakness is not thinking hard enough. A prime minister with any sense of past history would not have countenanced the stone's removal from Westminster in the first place; a prime minister with a sense of future history might have reflected upon the symbolism of his deed. Little that we do will last long, even if we are national leaders, but the Stone of Scone's return to Scotland is presumably irreversible (though it will come back to Westminster for coronations), and perhaps the act of Mr Major's hapless premiership which will endure longest is the symbol that he has left in the Abbey: an empty space where something solid ought to be.

Whereas John Major wanted to take something out of the Abbey, Tony Blair, his successor, wanted to put something in: himself. At the funeral of Princess Diana in 1997, he read a lesson, contrary to all constitutional precedent (imagine the fuss if Mrs Thatcher had tried that). The public seemed to like it at the time, but the heavy sentimentality with which he read from St Paul would probably gratify his enemies more than his friends if it were to be seen again now. However, he seems to have been pleased with the experiment: when the Queen Mother died in 2002, the *Spectator* reported that his office had pressed for the Prime Minister to have an enhanced role in the obsequies. This was ferociously denied by Downing Street, until it was proved to be true.

Diana's death is so recent and familiar an event and its significance so much wider than Westminster that I shall say little here, but the funeral had some features which deserve notice in any account of the Abbey's place in history. One is that the service itself was the still, central point in a sequence of movements: the slow, horse-drawn progress of the Princess's body from Kensington to Westminster, and its faster travel from Westminster to its final resting place in Northamptonshire. Indeed, the first part of these rituals revived a feature of medieval coronations: the procession across London, so that the citizenry as a whole might be part of the event. The progress of Diana's coffin was surely a matter of deliberate policy: her body had been lying in the Chapel Royal in St James's Palace, at no great distance from Westminster, but it was removed quietly in the night to Kensington Palace, so that its journey to the Abbey would take it right through the city's heart. It was shrewdly done – the first part of a catharsis which the Abbey would, more or less, complete.

Lord Spencer's address, publicly rebuking the royal family in their presence, was by any standards an extraordinary occasion. But it is the more striking from the place where it occurred – from the fact that the Queen was forced to hear herself attacked while facing the spot at which she had enjoyed her supreme moment of exaltation, forty-five years earlier. One might even think of Charles I, crowned in Westminster Abbey, tried in Westminster Hall across the street, and beheaded in Whitehall, up the street, though the reversal of fortune in that case was incomparably greater. The most extraordinary moment came at the end of the address, when the applause of the crowd outside, watching on television screens, was taken up by the congregation within. It is curious that modern technology thus restored the medieval participation of the populace in a royal event inside the church. But perhaps most lastingly memorable is the moment when tradition took over from innovation, choir from piano and microphone, as the Princess's coffin was borne slowly down the length of the nave to the incantatory music of John Tavener, straight as an arrow – except for the shuffle to avoid the Unknown Warrior. The Abbey had once more performed its role as a temple of reconciliation, absorbing Cool Britannia and popular heat into the rhythms of ritual performance.

The Queen Mother's funeral may seem, by contrast, to have been wholly traditional, but it was not: this was the first funeral in the Abbey of a king or queen for almost two and a half centuries. The Abbey is more wanted than ever as a theatre of national commemoration. And again it was a barometer: as the younger royals' decline in popularity moved the last royal wedding to Windsor, so conversely popular demand moved this occasion from Windsor to Westminster. The Abbey is designated, significantly, for the funerals of Prince Philip and the present Queen. The Queen Mother's obsequies joined Church and state, a union expressed through London's topography: Westminster Hall for the lying-in-state, the Abbey for the funeral itself. One and a quarter million people queued for five hours or more to see the lying-in-state; that means, of course, that some 58,000,000 citizens did not, but given the impracticality of attending for most people, it remains a formidable figure. The Abbey deals in continuities, but this death really did mark the end of something, and so it was strange to hear the celebrity historian in the BBC's commentary team regretting the recital of the Queen Mother's past titles near the end of the service. To the historical imagination, what titles! Empress of India! When Zita of Austria died in 1989, the papers said that she was the last empress in Europe. They were wrong; but how remarkable to think that the last empress survived into the twenty-first century. She had been at one time queen of a quarter of the world's population, queen over more people than any other woman in history; and that is something that can never come again. But the rituals of death do not change: once again the coffin carried down the nave, again the shuffle round the tomb of the Unknown Warrior; and there her funeral wreath was laid, where she had laid her bridal wreath, seventy-nine years before.

THE ABBEY NOW

Too many people, too many statues, too many chairs – visitors to the Abbey a few years back were likely to come away with an overwhelming sense of clutter. By the middle of the 1990s the Dean and Chapter had realised that something must be done to ease the scrum. Visitors to London had discovered that the nave was a good place to meet or wait, out of the rain (Pepys, user of the Abbey for less innocent assignations, would have understood). So the Dean and Chapter decided to charge for admission to any part of the building, attenuating the distinction between a public and a more enclosed part of the church which in one way or another had existed ever since its erection. Parties are taken in through the cloisters, entering in number by the route which Washington Irving once walked in solitude. Individual visitors come in through the north transept and have to see the sights in a prescribed order, passing along the north ambulatory, into Henry VII's Chapel and back down the south ambulatory to Poets' Corner. The nave comes at the end of the tour and is now the least densely populated part of the church – which feels slightly odd. The visitor is refreshed, however, by arriving at a more open and a spiritual space: two icons have been placed by pillars, and you may light a candle before them. The ordinary tourist is now excluded from the shrine, which can be visited only by previous arrangement. This was probably necessary, both to prevent congestion and to protect the fragile fabric, but it has meant that comparatively few people now see the most numinous space in London and some of the loveliest medieval statuary in existence. The effect, however, has been to make the shrine seem more than ever a holy of holies, inaccessible, its presence felt more than seen from the ambulatories below. And perhaps those who do get into the shrine may feel a little more like pilgrims reaching their destination.

The press of numbers is a fairly recent phenomenon. Betjeman could imagine a society lady during the Second World War dropping easily into the Abbey for a hobnob with the Deity:

> Let me take this other glove off
> As the *vox humana* swells,
> And the beauteous fields of Eden
> Bask beneath the Abbey bells.
> Here, where England's statesmen lie,
> Listen to a lady's cry.
>
> Gracious Lord, oh bomb the Germans,
> Spare their women for Thy Sake,
> And if that is not too easy
> We will pardon Thy Mistake.
> But, gracious Lord, whate'er shall be,
> Don't let anyone bomb me …
>
> Now I feel a little better,

What a treat to hear Thy Word,
Where the bones of leading statesmen
    Have so often been interr'd.
And now, dear Lord, I cannot wait
Because I have a luncheon date.

The satire is not subtle, but it does remind us that something has been lost, inevitably, now that it is no longer easy for a Londoner to slip into the church for a moment's solace or exaltation. But the Abbey has, in effect, compensated by taking its witness outside and enlarging its ecumenical mission even further. The west front is now literally an act of prayer, as to the left of the great door are conspicuously carved the words, 'May God grant to the living grace, to the departed rest, to the Church and the world peace and concord, and to us sinners eternal life.' The statues of Christian martyrs of the twentieth century are chosen to represent six continents and several denominations – Anglican, Roman Catholic, Orthodox, Lutheran, Baptist. The Abbey also tries to speak to all people, whatever their belief or unbelief; it is significant that this is where the annual Commonwealth service is held, an act of faith shared by the major world religions. Below the northern tower a stone commemorates 'the innocent victims of oppression, violence and war'. It is intended to speak to all humanity, and to act as a civilian counterpart to the Unknown Warrior beyond the doors. These acts of worship and memory seem to invite the passer-by inside, and it is a loss, undoubtedly, that such casual access is no longer possible; but the daily services are open to all, and hundreds come. The world changes, but as a building and as a community the Abbey continues to do what the Benedictines called the *opus Dei*, the work of God, to teach and preach and praise.

FURTHER READING

General and Miscellaneous

The literature on Westminster Abbey is large, and much is of dauntingly high quality. The official history is Edward Carpenter (ed.), *A House of Kings* (London, revised edition, 1972). A more popular account, admirably written and with good illustrations, is *Kingdom, Power and Glory*, 'a historical guide' by John Field (London, third edition, 2002). The Abbey's excellent official guide, *Westminster Abbey*, is especially informative on the tombs and monuments. Christopher Wilson and others, *Westminster Abbey* (New Bell's Cathedral Guides, London, 1986) covers most aspects of the Abbey. The long history of the Abbey's conservation is illuminated by Thomas Cocke, *900 Years: The Restorations of Westminster Abbey* (London, 1995), with contributions by Donald Buttress, the surveyor who directed the most recent restoration. James Wilkinson, *Westminster Abbey: 1000 Years of Music and Pageant* (London, 2003) gives a lively account of the Abbey's musical history, and is again very well illustrated; it also comes with a CD. A substantial booklet, *Stained Glass of Westminster Abbey* (2002), mostly depicting glass of the nineteenth and twentieth centuries, opens up an often neglected period and area of ecclesiastical art; the text is by Christine Reynolds.

London 6: Westminster (London, 2003) by Simon Bradley and Nikolaus Pevsner, a massive revision and expansion of Pevsner's original work in his Buildings of England series, is a superb source for both information and interpretation; it includes more than 100 close-packed pages on the Abbey complex alone, as well as other material relevant to its physical and social setting.

Westminster Abbey, published by the Annenberg School Press in 1972, is a luxury volume brought about by the enthusiasm of Walter Annenberg, American ambassador in London at the time (his name appears as a benefactor in a window of Henry VII's Chapel). Various luminaries are on display: there are chapters by A. L. Rowse and John Pope-Hennessy in characteristic mode (on 'the Abbey in the history of the nation' and the sculpture respectively), and atmospheric pieces by John Betjeman and Kenneth Clark. Some of the photography is excellent, some below par.

⧗

Scholarly study of the Abbey's fabric goes back to the seventeenth century, and older works are often well worth seeking out. Sumptuous and evocative engravings are supplied in E. W. Brayley and J. P. Neale, *The History and Antiquities of the Abbey Church of St Peter, Westminster* (London, 1818–23). Two surveyors who wrote about the building are Gilbert Scott, *Gleanings from Westminster Abbey* (Oxford, second edition, 1863), and W. R. Lethaby, *Westminster Abbey and the King's Craftsmen* (London, 1906) and *Westminster Abbey Re-Examined* (London, 1925). A. P. Stanley, *Historical Memorials of Westminster Abbey* (London, fifth edition, 1882) is a treasure chest of antiquarian information, as well as a glimpse into the character of a famous dean. Another insider's account comes from Jocelyn Perkins, *Westminster Abbey: its Worship and Ornaments* (London, 3 vols., 1938–52), eccentric, not wholly likeable, but full of diverse information.

The Medieval Building

Studies of Gothic architecture are beyond counting. Jean Bony, *The English Decorated Style: Gothic Architecture Transformed, 1250–1350* (Oxford, 1979), sets the Abbey and other English buildings of its time in the context of the French architecture that came before it. George Zarnecki contributes a chapter on the Abbey's art and architecture to the Annenberg School Press volume described above. See too the relevant chapters, by H. M. Colvin, in volumes 1 and 3 of the *History of the King's Works* (London, vols., 1963-82). Paul Binski, *Westminster Abbey and the Plantagenets: Kingship and the Representation of Power, 1200-1400* (New Haven and London, 1995), is a brilliant study with a distinctive case to argue; it investigates both the architecture of the Abbey and its ideology and historical setting. The many photographs are chosen with great intelligence. Henry VII's Chapel gets detailed scholarly scrutiny in Tim Tatton-Brown and Richard Mortimer (eds.), *Westminster Abbey: The Lady Chapel of Henry VII* (Woodbridge, Suffolk, 2003). For the mosaic floors see Lindy Grant and Richard Mortimer (eds.) *Westminster Abbey: The Cosmati Pavements* (Aldershot, 2002).

According to Binski, 'Westminster Abbey preserves more by way of medieval archival material than do some smaller nation states.' Most of it is still housed in the Muniment Room, and some of it in a plain twelfth-century oak chest of astonishing dimensions. The Muniment Room is an enthralling space: enclosed within the west aisle of the south transept, some thirty feet up, it offers enchanting vistas of a stone forest of columns and arches, past the crossing and the sanctuary into the ambulatory and the chapels beyond. This archive forms the basis for Barbara Harvey's great studies, *Westminster Abbey and Its Estates in the Middle Ages* (Oxford, 1977) and *Living and Dying in England, 1100–1540* (Oxford, 1993), which vividly re-creates the monks' existence. For the Abbey in relation to the medieval town around it, see also Gervase Rosser, *Medieval Westminster: 1200–1540* (Oxford, 1989).

The Sculpture

Lawrence Stone, *Sculpture in Britain: The Middle Ages* (Harmondsworth, 1955), and Phillip Lindley, *Gothic to Renaissance: Essays on Sculpture in England* (Stamford, 1995) discuss the Westminster sculpture and set it in context. Margaret Whinney, *Sculpture in Britain, 1530 to 1830* (Harmondsworth, 1964; second edition, rev. John Physick, 1988), provides a comprehensive if somewhat withering survey of its subject. Katharine Esdaile's pioneering study of Roubiliac (London, 1928) is now mostly superseded by David Bindman and Malcolm Baker, *Roubiliac and the Eighteenth-century Monument: Sculpture as Theatre* (New Haven and London, 1995), a book which casts light on the setting of sculpture in the Abbey as well as the works themselves. It also offers new colour photographs of all Roubiliac's church monuments. A fair number of the Abbey's later monuments are illustrated in Benedict Read, *Victorian Sculpture* (New Haven and London, 1982).

DESCRIPTIONS AND EVOCATIONS

Most of my quotations will be found easily enough by those who want to chase them up. Addison's meditations on Westminster Abbey come in the *Spectator*, no. 26, and I have also drawn on two other of his *Spectator* essays. Defoe's words come from *A Tour through the Whole Island of Great Britain*. Voltaire discusses the Abbey in his *Letters concerning the English Nation*. The letter of Burke which I quote is of disputed authenticity. Washington Irving's piece appears in *The Sketch Book of Geoffrey Crayon, Gent*. Macaulay made his famous comment on the Abbey near the end of his essay on Warren Hastings. Pugin's praises and fulminations come in his *Contrasts*. For Hawthorne I have used *The English Notebooks*, ed. Randall Stewart (New York, 1941). Henry James included 'Browning in Westminster Abbey' in his *English Hours*.

CEREMONY AND COMMEMORATION

Dean Stanley is very fully memorialised in a two-volume *Life and Correspondence* by Rowland Prothero (London, 1893). A shorter study is Peter Hammond, *Dean Stanley of Westminster* (Worthing, 1987).

Newspapers (such as *The Times*) and illustrated magazines (such as the *Sphere* and the *Illustrated London News*) give a good sense of the royal ceremonials of the twentieth century and the spirit in which they were taken at the time. The story of the Tomb of the Unknown Warrior is traced by Bob Bushaway in Roy Porter (ed.), *Myths of the English* (Cambridge, 1992). For coronations especially I have also drawn upon the official and other biographies of monarchs: Sidney Lee on Edward VII, Giles St Aubyn on the same, Harold Nicolson on George V, Kenneth Rose on the same, John Wheeler-Bennett on George VI, Ben Pimlott on the present Queen. The most vivid account of Edward VII's coronation is by A. C. Benson: see David Newsome (ed.), *Edwardian Excursion: From the Diaries of A.C. Benson, 1898–1904* (London, 1981). J. G. Lockhart's life of Cosmo Gordon Lang (London, 1949) is illuminating on the coronation of George VI, and Chips Channon's diaries cast an amusing eye on the two most recent coronations (Robert Rhodes James (ed.), *Chips: The Diaries of Sir Henry Channon* (London, 1967)).

The huge literature on coronation extends beyond Westminster Abbey, and indeed far beyond Britain. Modern coronations and other royal ceremonies in Britain get shrewd examination from David Cannadine in Eric Hobsbawm and Terence Ranger (eds.) *The Invention of Tradition*, (Cambridge, 1983). An interesting contemporary analysis of Elizabeth II's coronation is that by Edward Shils and Michael Young in *Sociological Review*. vol. 1, no. 2, 1953, pp. 68–81. This produced a riposte from N. Birnbaum, published in the same journal two years later: the coronation was not the expression of national solidarity that Shils and Young supposed; for a truly unified country one must look instead to socialist Yugoslavia.

Lastly

The best way to understand the Abbey's spiritual life is to experience it; there is normally at least one service each day. Michael Mayne's *Pray, Love, Remember* (London, 1998) is a devotional book, each chapter based upon a particular part of the Abbey, by a former dean.

ILLUSTRATIONS

Plan   2
Westminster Abbey (from Simon Bradley and Nikolaus
Pevsner, *London 6: Westminster*, 2003)

Endpapers
Two views of the nave of Westminster Abbey, from R.
Ackermann, *The History of the Abbey Church of St Peter's
Westminster* (1812)

ILLUSTRATION CREDITS

Dean and Chapter of Westminster: 1, 2, 5, 6, 7, 8, 9, 10, 11, 12,
13, 18, 19, 20, 22, 23; Fotomas Index UK: endpapers; John
Crook: 4; National Monuments Record/Royal Commission
on the Historical Monuments of England: 3, 14, 16, 17; PA
Photos: 24; Yale University Press: plan.

While every effort has been made to contact copyright-
holders of illustrations, the author and publishers would be
grateful for information about any illustrations where they
have been unable to trace them, and would be glad to make
amendments in further editions.

ACKNOWLEDGEMENTS

My pleasure in preparing and writing this book has been enhanced by the friendly help that many people have given me. From the moment I confessed to her that I was writing a book about the Abbey, Barbara Harvey has been exceptionally generous with advice and encouragement; she also read a draft, pointed out errors and showed me how to make improvements. I have had a warm welcome at the Abbey library, and as warmly thank Richard Mortimer, Keeper of the Muniments, Christine Reynolds, Assistant Keeper, and Tony Trowles, Librarian of the Abbey. The Very Reverend Wesley Carr, Dean of Westminster, and the Very Reverend Michael Mayne, emeritus Dean, have both given me their time, their hospitality and the wisdom of their experience. Mary Beard not only persuaded me to write the book but read it in draft, as did Peter Carson; their counsel has bettered it. Lesley Levene was an acute and tactful copy-editor. For permission to quote from John Betjeman, *In Westminster Abbey*, I thank John Murray Publishers. My thanks too for help of one kind or another to Simon Bradley, Will Francis, Christine Gerrard, Carol Heaton, Clive Holmes, Neil Hynd, Viola Jones, Tom Keymer and Ann Schofield.

In a book without footnotes, it is sometimes necessary to

present probabilities as undoubted facts or to choose between competing accounts without explanation. But I am likely to have made mistakes which cannot be excused on such grounds, and these are my own responsibility.

INDEX

WONDERS OF THE WORLD

This is a small series of books, under the general editorship of Mary Beard, that will focus on some of the world's most famous sites or monuments.

Already available

Mary Beard: *The Parthenon*
Robert Irwin: *The Alhambra*
Simon Goldhill: *The Temple of Jerusalem*